Arabia Felix
A Land of Builders

Photographs: Ennio Vicario

Published in the United States of America in 1977 by:

*R*IZZOLI INTERNATIONAL PUBLICATIONS, INC.
712 Fifth Avenue/New York 10019

Originally published as *Yemen, paese di costruttori*
© 1977 by Electa Editrice, Milano

Library of Congress Catalog Card Number: 76-11995
ISBN: 0-8478-0050-4

Printed in Italy by Fantonigrafica, Venice

Design Diego Birelli

Translated by Daphne Newton

Paolo Costa
and Ennio Vicario

Arabia Felix A Land of Builders

Though an Arabist I have to admit that of all the Arab countries I have visited it has never been my good fortune to set foot in the mother peninsula, and the only view I have had of the fantastic architecture of the Yemen has been in illustrated form. Yet I have been requested to introduce this fine book, which will be for many the revelation of an unknown world.

I have accepted the invitation because even without direct, visual experience anyone with the slightest knowledge of Islamic history and civilization will be able to appreciate the past and present role of the country portrayed in these pictures. Even before Islam there flourished a most remarkable civilization of settlers and farmers in the ancient world, guardian of an immense heritage, versed in religious cults, commerce and artistic activities that were almost unknown to the rest of Arabia. Then, within Islam, a secluded world emerged, mindful of its ancient greatness, conserving those characteristics of civilization and culture of which it and the other Moslem countries were fully conscious. The traditions of ancient Yemenite building and fortifications, of topography, dialects, customs and poetry had, in mediaeval Yemen, renowned patrons, the most notable being the great al-Hamdani (10th century A.D.) whom general Arab-Moslem culture regarded with awe and reverence. This extreme consciousness of regional identity, favoured by physical and historical conditions has enabled Yemen to preserve that archaic physiognomy, which to this day fascinates its few Western visitors and which even from afar exerts an irresistible charm through these illustrations.

We are grateful to Paolo Costa and Ennio Vicario, an eminent archaeologist and a photographer-publicist, for capturing this world and transmitting its charm. In the general outline on building techniques Costa's long experience of the Yemen prepares the reader for the uniqueness of modern Yemenite architecture (modern not meaning, as elsewhere the destruction of the ancient, but its harmonious preservation and continuance) and using illustrations of four typical towns (Sa'dah, Manākha, Zabīd and San'a), guides him to a greater appreciation of the urban and artistic traits of Arabia Felix today. With his camera Vicario has expertly captured for us those shapes, of nature and humble, friendly humanity, which an unbroken tradition has handed down to us uncontaminated (just think of the Americanization of town-planning in neighbouring Saudi-Arabia, not to mention the Holy City of Mecca itself). Glancing through this book, even the least acquainted with Arab-Islamic civilization will feel a breath of the authentic, together with the flavour of the far away and unknown, in forms of sometimes amazing beauty. The Arabist and scholar of Islam will be able to enjoy a deeper understanding of its history and subtle, complex associations. He will see Shānfara, the robber poet of Arabian paganism, profiled in the solitude he evokes on a mountain of the High Yemen and the Persians of Wahriz, drawing their long-bows against the ephemeral Abyssinian conquerors in aid of the Yemeni nobility and the first groups of Moslems praying on the very spot where the Great Mosque of San'a now stands. He will listen to the age-old silence, broken nowadays by the roar of jets overhead and echoing rifleshots, which have recently started to undermine the feudal structure of the country, but which hopefully, will not prevent it preserving the enchanting appearance shown here. Is it possible to achieve modern development without destroying the material and spiritual legacy of one's ancestors? This we would wish for Arabia Felix, from the magic circle of these pictures, and would like to thank those who have worked so hard and risked so much to present it to us.

Francesco Gabrieli

1. Cultivated terraces and settlement of the western slope of the Yemenite plateau.
2. Qariat al Naqīl, ancient settlement by the Islah pass.
3. Dwellings and cultivated land along the Wadi Dhahr. ▷

This book is the result of two distinct experiences, but a common interest in architecture. Ennio Vicario, in a brief but extremely active stay in Yemen, experienced the intense emotion of encountering a world full of new and rich sensations, and satisfied the interest aroused by every detail and every aspect of that world by taking thousands of photographs. I had more time and opportunity to enter into contact with deeper-lying aspects of Yemenite civilization, partly through the nature of my job itself. In the text, however, I have tried to adhere as closely as possible to Vicario's kind of experience. I know I am interpreting his thought in saying that we wanted to give a presentation of Yemeni architecture in which much was left at the stage of intuition, or rough impression. Hence the book is really the
result of collaboration: Vicario's pictures and my text complement each other, so as to give a first reaction to Yemeni architecture. If the photographs succeed in whetting the appetite for greater knowledge and the text stimulates correction and criticism, and encourages a deeper study, much of our aim will have been accomplished. The outline on Yemeni architecture is certainly not intended to give more than a first approach to almost unknown material.
So few Yemeni monuments have been studied or brought to public notice that we have avoided using any of the graphic material so far available, as it would have proved entirely inadequate even for an elementary presentation of the various problems. Instead, we have relied exclusively on photography.
The texts on the four cities chosen to
show different ways of building, and the relative illustrations, are intended to be an impressionistic sketch rather than a realistic picture. The brief history of the country is only a compilation we felt would be of use to the reader in understanding Yemeni civilization.
In the course of this summary words or items that might be incomprehensible to the general reader are explained or described.

P.M. Costa

The authors are grateful to Dr Germana Graziosi Costa for her valuable assistance in editing the texts; Dr. Giovanni Firmian for his friendly help during their travels in Yemen; architect Leonardo Costa for drawing up the archaelogical map. They also wish to mention how much the work owes to the kind hospitality of the Yemeni people and to the support of the local authorities.

THE ARCHITECTURE OF THE YEMEN

Looking down from the aeroplane for the first time at the Yemen, its terraces marking every feature of the landscape like the contour-lines of a gigantic relief map, I was struck by how man had carved out this corner of Arabia, turning it gradually and evidently over thousands of years, into an almost artificial country. After travelling in hundreds of directions through the endless valleys of this tiny country, the first impression persists: the Yemen has been made by its inhabitants. They have not, however, carved it out, but rather built it, placing stone on stone so that building has gradually become as natural to them as breathing. This wonderful, innate tendency to build is the most striking aspect of the Yemeni people, even from one's very first contact with the country. The Yemeni plateau is usually presented as the only vast region of the Arabian peninsula where particularly propitious living conditions have favoured the establishment of sedentary, farming populations since remote times. This is undoubtedly true. But in presenting the favourable environmental conditions of "Arabia Felix," not enough stress has been laid on the fact that it would have been almost impossible to extend arable land without terracing, and that without irrigation systems, the fruits of cultivation would have been negligible.

Rainfall is seasonal in the Yemen, torrential and of brief duration: without suitable levelling and soil retention or systematic collection and distribution of the waters the benefit of the rains would have been greatly reduced. Thus the civilization of Southern Arabia seems to have been essentially one of farmer-builders. To understand the earliest origins of Yemenite architecture it is useful to consider how the extensive and, at times, gigantic works for collecting and distributing the water were made possible. These works represent not only huge displacements of earth and of rock, and millions of cubic metres of stonework, but also imply remarkable technical knowledge for soil levelling, canal planning and water collecting, and require advanced technological experience of materials, especially for the preparation of hydraulic mortar and plaster. The high degree of technical ability attained by the peoples of Southern Arabia in the field of agriculture must, together with the caravan trade, be considered one of the chief reasons for the prosperity of the Southern Arabian kingdoms. The immense archaeological heritage of Southern Arabia is still practically unknown, and very little research has been done on scientific lines. The brief excavations at Huqqah Hamdan, Hureidha, Timna and Ma'rib have supplied very modest data to the knowledge of pre-Islamic religious architecture and tell us practically nothing about civil building.

Here we shall examine modern architecture in the Yemen. In chronological terms this means from the early centuries of Islam, since some of the most ancient mosques still in use date back to this period, up to a few decades ago when, with the importation of new building materials, local architecture began to lose the natural pureness it had kept for centuries. Religious buildings are particularly important for the study of architecture for two main reasons. They tend to maintain a fundamental continuity, even after restorations, enlargements and reconstructions, and an analysis of their building history is often facilitated by the availability of written sources. The architecture which is still in use. today is represented by the house, and is the most typical and interesting expression of Yemenite architecture. In no other country in the Middle East have civil buildings survived so conspicuously, keeping their characteristics intact through the centuries. And it is most unusual that these are not aulic buildings but ordinary houses: in the Yemen there are no hovels, but there are no real mansions either, to compare, for instance, with the Umayad castles or Caliphs' palaces. It should also be noted that there is little difference between rural and urban architecture, if any at all. A vivid oral tradition, and even family documents, provide useful elements for the dating of houses that may be five or six hundred years old.

What is most striking about Yemenite architecture is the mixture of very advanced technology and clearly makeshift arrangements. Comparing it with European architecture the absence of any real school, such as that of the Renaissance, is evident. There is instead an excellent craftsmanship which has enabled them to build with the constructional freedom of the Comacine masters. A comparison with Northern Italian Romanesque art must of course be taken in its widest sense. There is, however, in both types of architecture a common aesthetic value in the pronounced constructional freedom expressed mainly through a refusal to organize the various elements, whether distributive or decorative, into any symmetrical composition. As we have said, at our present stage of research it is very difficult to tell how much of pre-Islamic constructional method has survived in the oldest existing mediaeval buildings and to what extent continuity of pre-Islamic building tradition is to be found in later periods. Certainly in both mediaeval and modern architecture at least the technique, if not the decoration, still shows signs of having very ancient origins and of a millennial experience.

The architecture of a country as ethnically and geographically mixed as the Yemen can only be studied by taking into account the variations in its climate and morphology. The link considered to exist in general between architecture and the environment is all the more valid

and significant in the Yemen where the geographical differences are more distinctly emphasized by a variety of contributory causes: historical, as regards the political divisions; religious, on account of the various Islamic sects, not to mention the Jewish communities; and environmental-economic, especially where the difficulties of transportation are concerned. Political divisions often imposed differences in technique and taste, religious divisions determined voluntary choice of building plans and decoration which sometimes assume an almost emblematic value. Transportation difficulties, especially on the hard mountain trails which until a few years ago formed a high percentage of communications in the country, discouraged the use of heavy materials beyond the area of production or extraction, thus augmenting the effect of natural choice of familiar materials. And finally the climate varies so much that it must be included among the decisive factors in creating architectural differences.

In order to study Yemenite architecture in relationship to the chief geographical regions, a distinction must be made between the rugged mountain plateau, reaching heights of up to 4000 metres but deeply furrowed by extremely fertile valleys; the middle plateau and the slopes down towards the desert, which are steppe-like and arid; and the lowland, or Tihāma, a dry sandy coastal strip, with a wide belt of fertile land up to the foot of the mountains.

The distinguishing feature of the Yemenite houses of the plateau and valleys right down to the coastal strip along the Red Sea, is their remarkable height. This obviously posed great technical problems which seem to have been brilliantly, often daringly, solved, apparently relying more on flashes of genius than calculation, irrespective of the material used. The stone and brick houses in San'a, Hajjah, 'Amrān,

Dhamar, Yarīm, Ibb, Ta'izz and Manākha rise four or five storeys above ground-level on average as do the mud brick or pisé houses on the inland plateau, which we also find at Sa'dah, and in the areas of the Jawf and Ma'rib.

In stone houses the foundations are not usually very deep and are made of rough-hewn blocks of basalt, which are mortared together with a mixture of clay and stone chips. These base walls stand about a metre above ground-level and owing to the nature of the stone, which tends to chip, it is not worked to a smooth finish. They look rather rustic, and the aesthetic result effectively stresses the function of this part of the building. Above the foundations the outside walls of the house stand at least two storeys high, in squared tufa or limestone, giving it an extremely solid and powerful character, due also to the few and tiny windows. The ground and first floors, except when used as shops are stables and storehouses, which require continuous ventilation but little light. For this reason as well as for security, the window openings on this floor are mere slits and this part of the building takes on the severe aspect of a fortress. On the second floor there is usually a kitchen with a large brick fireplace, the women's and children's rooms and a bathroom. The windows are again relatively small. On the external walls there is a series of openings to let the smoke out and a latticed, stone box which allows the air to circulate and where jars of drinking water and perishable foods are kept. After this, according to the size of the family, there are one or more floors, with bedrooms and living-rooms lit by spacious windows which are relatively high up so as to ensure privacy. The large houses have, in addition to this, a fairly big room called diwān or makān al kebīr, which serves as a communal living-room, where meals are taken,

4. Houses in old San'a.
5. Stone mashrabiyah intended for water jars.

and relations or close acquaintances received. There is also a room for the exclusive use of the head of the family, and here the objects and furnishings of greatest value are kept. It is in this room that the books and documents of the family are jealously guarded. These sometimes include important collections handed down from father to son, often containing ancient manuscripts and rare books of great historical interest. They are the private libraries for which the Yemen is famous, a mine of research material not yet explored scientifically. The top storey is usually occupied by a huge single room with large windows close to floor level on at least three sides. It is called māfrej or māndhar (belvedere), and is a large living-room used by the men for the afternoon siesta, where they chew qat, smoke the mada'ah (water pipe) and receive guests.

The māfrej is not only the heart of the Yemenite house but the centre of an intense social, cultural and political life, associated with the chewing of qat which assumes an almost ritual value. The top storeys of the house are amply lit by externally and internally decorated windows, above which there are either small circular openings with alabaster panes or lunettes with stucco tracery and multicoloured glass. On both sides of these openings there are small slits which serve exclusively for ventilation.

The windows are nearly always protected externally by a richly decorated wooden ledge and by shutters, which, before glass was imported about two centuries ago, was the only way of closing them. Bathrooms are set between floors usually from the second storey up: excrement drains are internal while drains for liquids are channelled in simply framed open grooves down the outside walls of the building into catchpits. These drains, though undoubtedly unpleasant, are usually situated on the lateral walls and are often embellished by the ingenious design of the frames silhouetted against the dark stone. The ceilings are formed of layers of branches spread with almost a foot of clay and supported by thick wooden beams. These are stripped tree-trunks which even under the thick clay plaster and whitewash, display their bulky forms and it is this very irregularity which gives the ceilings their unmistakable and most attractive appearance.

The staircase, wide, but with steep risers, rests on four ramps for each floor and is built around an impressive central pier. It is ventilated and dimly lit by small window embrasures without glass. The Yemeni house on the plateau is characterized, therefore, by a firm sound base reaching a height of 6-8 metres, where the only large opening is the door. Above this there is nearly

always a depressed arch surmounted by a stilted arch. In the resulting lunette there are several small arched openings which ensure ventilation in the rather damp and dark entranceway.

On this solid base stands the upper part of the building, which is made of limestone or baked bricks, and very occasionally of large mud bricks. As mentioned previously this part of the building, which might be defined as the real habitation, is provided with many wide windows, some beautifully decorated. It is not unusual, especially in San'a, to find terraced roofs with a series of small arches across the façade. There are frequent variations on this type of tower-house, with perhaps two or more articulated buildings forming small courtyards and enclosed by a perimeter wall. These individual buildings in a one-family complex are sometimes linked at the upper storeys, and often represent different stages of construction, determined by the changing needs or economic possibilities of the family. It is rare for these successive stages to have a negative effect, as the complex is usually put together with an amazing harmony of volume and decoration. In houses with a garden, and in the large country houses, there is nearly always a māfrej on the ground floor consisting of a rectangular room with large windows on one of the long sides looking on to a portico. This room, which can also be an isolated building, faces the garden and usually has a fountain in front of it. This type of māfrej may substitute the makān al kebīr, but more often is in addition to it.

The most recent type of house, particularly frequent today on the outskirts of the towns, consists of a single storey. A large entrance forms the axis of the house, with rooms on both sides. These houses, surrounded by an enclosed garden, lack the stables and stores associated with the traditional tower-house, and all the rooms have large windows. It is the home of a different kind of society, where the living style is no longer patriarchal: the stables have been replaced by garages, the stores are unnecessary because liquid gas has taken the place of firewood; supplies are bought daily according to need, and there are no more grindstones. The latticed box for keeping water and hanging the meat has been replaced by the refrigerator. The ground floor windows have to be barred since they afford little protection.

The Yemenite house is usually without a cellar, except in the case of the Jewish house, where there is always at least one basement room. These were mainly used for making and storing alcoholic drinks, authorization for which the Jews have always received from the Imams provided the alcohol was for their own consumption. But there is another reason for cellars in the Jewish house as well. They needed to make the best possible use of the inside of the building, as it was limited in height above ground level by precise laws based on the principles expressed in the Koran (Sura 9/29) that "the house of unbelievers should be lower and smaller than those of the Moslems." Apart from this height limit the remarkable lack of building space in the ghetto itself must be taken into account. Inside its wall the ghetto obviously could not spread as it should have done to keep pace with the gradual but steady growth of a population engaged in retailing and crafts. This growth was, in any case, linked with the fluctuation of the city's population in general, which tended to be on the increase rather than decrease, at least in the large towns. The search for building space inside the Jewish quarters is also proved by the characteristically narrow streets, especially in the ancient ghettoes still within the city walls. Jewish traders also had to find storage space in their homes for their merchandise as, unlike

13. Sa'dah, upper level courtyard of a house in the Jewish quarter.
14. Detail of a carved wooden door panel, Sa'dah.
15. Zabīd, interior of an inn.

Moslem merchants, they had no common warehouses organized and protected by the various guilds. Other characteristics of Jewish houses in the Yemen are the levels of the various rooms, differing according to their use and determined by an exasperated search for space on account of the strict height limits, a huge terrace on the penultimate floor, with rooms opening off it to form a kind of elevated courtyard for religious and practical usage; and the remarkable wealth of internal decoration, perhaps a reaction to the severe exterior of the building imposed by law.

Of these characteristics, the most striking is undoubtedly the terrace-courtyard. Various explanations have been given for it, and above all the religious one. During the so-called "tabernacle" festivities celebrated for a week in September or October, Jews were supposed to take their meals and spend the nights in a room covered only by leafy branches or matting. Attention has already been drawn to the necessity of making the most of the available space in Jewish houses, so it is not surprising to find a place suitable for the religious requirements on such an important festival serving the double purpose of a courtyard. The reason for raising this courtyard to an upper floor may be explained both by the need to have a lighter, more spacious and attractive environment, which would be difficult to achieve on the ground floor owing to the narrowness of the roads, and by the importance of providing this part of the house with sufficient intimacy.

After the famous mass exodus organized by the Israeli authorities in 1950-51, the Jewish population in the Yemen, once substantial, was reduced to a few thousand inhabitants in villages to the north of the country, where they have always been on good terms with the Moslems. Now that the big city ghettoes

(especially at San'a, Ta'izz, Dhamar, Manākha, 'Amrān, Sa'dah) no longer have a raison d'être, this type of architecture is unfortunately beginning to disappear. Even though it reflected the peculiar needs of an ethno-religious minority, it must, on the strength of an objective analysis of general building technique, be considered an integral part of the Yemeni architecture.

There is hardly any furniture in the traditional Yemeni house. Tables are not needed because every activity, from cooking to reading and writing, is done on the floor. Instead of wardrobes and cupboards there are chests and built-in closets. On average there are two to a room, with coloured-glass doors. In the head of the family's room there may be a squat writing-desk with cushions for the user to sit on. Living-rooms and bedrooms are one and the same. By day one sits on mattresses covered with woollen mats or carpets. They are placed along the walls and have large cushions. Other cushions are arranged perpendicularly against the wall to be used as arm rests. At night these cushions are replaced by pillows. Beds are fairly rare on the plateau, but are found more frequently down in the Tihāma, where they replace ground-mattresses even for use during the day. They consist of a large wickerwork frame raised on legs, often over a metre high.

The fastenings on all the wooden furnishings throughout the house are beautifully and often very finely worked: especially the great heavy main door, with an iron knocker, the inner doors opening into the most important rooms and the shutters on the upper floors. The Yemen craftsmen are often not only expert wood-carvers but also surprisingly inventive, as can be seen in the case of this folding stair. Internal decoration finds rich and

16, 17. San'a, folding staircase of Dar al Sa'adah.
(Palace of Imam Yahya).
18. Māfrej of a house in San'a (Bait al Watāri).
19. Dar el Shukr (National Museum of the Yemen).

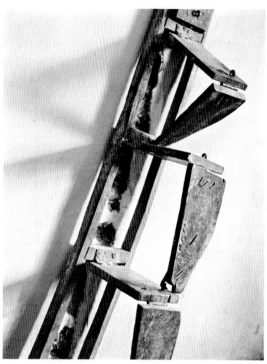

sometimes extravagant expression, especially in the reception rooms in the gypsum plaster shelves that run round all the walls at a height of about two metres. This is perhaps the most typical decorative element in the interior of Yemeni houses. The bare white walls are relieved here and there by recesses which frame cupboards and doors. The shelves, plain and linear in design but with ornately carved and fretted supports, break up the blank expanse of the wall. They are about 20 cm deep, and are used for small functional and decorative objects that enhance the room by standing out against the light-coloured walls. In the richer houses the walls are decorated by floral designs or quotations from the Koran, often in very elaborate calligraphy and in high relief.

The external decoration on houses in the plateau area is usually simple but quite striking: all the mouldings and decorations in relief are highlighted by a coat of whitewash, which is touched up periodically.
A fairly frequent motif, especially in large buildings and mosques, is the chromatic contrast between the sand-coloured limestone and dark-grey tufa. The latter is used for quoins and roof edges, door and window lintels and frames, horizontal mouldings marking the floors, and cornices. These skeletal elements of the building stand out against the light-coloured walls, emphasizing the structure and yet at the same time giving it a surprisingly light appearance which breaks up the monotony of the limestone and the heavy mass of the building.

One of the fundamental factors in the plateau architecture examined here is the technique of stone cutting. The blocks used in the pre-Islamic period were perfectly squared on five faces,

thus requiring a great deal of work in order to prepare the perfect blocks necessary for the assembling of the wall. Since the Middle Ages a different technique has been widely used. The blocks are roughly hewn and then squared and faced only on one side, which is smoothed with a heavy adze-like hammer. This way of preparing the stone block requires just as much skill but less precision and working time, thus enabling the work to be done quickly and well. The blocks are carefully fitted only on the side that shows, and fixed in position on the inside with stone chippings and mortar.

While the inner side of the masonry which is levelled off with a thick layer of clay and finished with plaster, is made up of uneven blocks and stone chippings, the outer face of the wall looks as if it were of ashlar construction with joints seldom exceeding a millimetre. This building technique which has been used since the Middle Ages for the houses was already employed in pre-Islamic times for large structures such as dams, city walls and fortifications. It was very different of course from the use of completely squared blocks which were reserved for temples, royal palaces and other important buildings. Even with our as yet limited knowledge of pre-Islamic architecture we can state fairly confidently that as there are only few remains of private houses among the ruins of the Sabaean cities, they must have been built with perishable material. So modern Yemeni architecture represents a remarkable social conquest through the adoption of one particular way of building.

In these brief notes on the architecture of the plateau, mention should be made of two types of public works typical of this area: the semsarah and the cistern. Comparable to the Middle-Eastern caravanserai the semsarah appears in two variants. In the towns it is a large, complex structure, built to provide shelter for men, animals and caravan merchandise when they come to town on business and may stay for a certain number of days. In the large cities there are a large number of semsarah and they usually stand on the edge of the suq. A large room at the end of the building is for the beasts of burden, and small rooms open off the main entrance for the men of the caravan to eat, sleep and receive customers in. For an exceptionally important semsarah this basic plan may be enlarged to two or more floors above ground-level with the ground floor reserved for the animals. Near the door is the fireplace where the caretakers prepare tea, qishr (an infusion of coffee-bean husks) and the live coals for the mada'ah (water pipe). In regard to building technique, the city semsarah has no particular characteristics: in comparison with private houses one can observe a certain crudeness and lack of gypsum plaster finishings. Along the caravan routes another type of semsarah can be seen, properly known as sabīl, or sakf. Smaller, simple in the extreme, it is meant exclusively for brief caravan stops. It is usually built voluntarily by the community or, in a few rare cases, by private individuals who offer them in the name of the traditional Moslem assistance to travellers. Rather numerous, the sabīl are a typical feature of the Yemeni countryside. The building is megalithic in type; the dry-wall construction consists of one huge rectangular room with an arched entrance, usually on one of the short sides. Heavy transverse arches hold up the roof structure which consists of short, roughly squared stone beams. The roofing is completed with broad unworked stones, covered with a thick layer of earth. The inner walls are sometimes finished with a rough coating of clay plaster. As the sabīl is unguarded, it is completely devoid of portable furnishings; there is not even a door, so the entrance way is always

placed on the most sheltered side of the building to avoid the strongest and coldest winds.

There is often a cistern by the sabīl for the animals to drink from, which is also used for the ritual ablutions that the travellers perform before praying. Occasionally there is no cistern, especially in areas where the sabīl are particularly numerous; evidently some are only meant for brief stops, or shelter from short storms or showers. The cisterns are therefore an accessory rather than a basic requirement, partly because it is only for short periods in the year that there is enough rain to fill them.

In the plain between 'Amrān and Reidah, north of San'a, there are a few examples of underground sabīl. In order to save on transportation of stones, which are scarce in the area, the room is scooped out of the ground for almost its whole length; only the front part and the entrance are built in the usual way with large blocks of stone. This part of the sabīl slopes gradually downwards in order to meet the lower section below ground level. Caravan semsarah were built in the Yemen until a few decades ago, but motorization has rendered this type of shelter unnecessary today. It would be practically impossible to work out the chronology of the sabīl, but it certainly belongs to a most ancient tradition.

As regards the walls, the sabīl can only be compared with the supporting walls of terraced fields. The roof may perhaps be compared with the exclusively stone roofing found in the Nabataean area and in the Parthian centres of Northern Mesopotamia. This is not surprising if one considers that the sabīl are buildings which grew up along caravan routes belonging to the great roadway system of the Middle East.

As we have said, the cisterns, and all the works for retaining and distributing

water in general, are of ancient origin; this is proved for the pre-Islamic period by the magnificent hydraulic engineering works in the Southern Arabian kingdoms. There are still numerous cisterns on the plateau where natural drainage basins and the sloping ground allow the rain water to be collected. There are many examples of large pre-Islamic cisterns restored and maintained up to the present day, like that of Tayyibah, near San'a; as well as smaller, more recent tanks which are used primarily for irrigation purposes and are still to be found in the countryside and in the villages.

Mention has been made of the variety of materials used in the architecture of the plateau and that of the north and east regions; this, however, only gives rise to remarkable differences in the decoration, as the building itself is almost the same in both areas. Sa'dah and San'a provide the most notable examples of the two main variants. Sa'dah, completely built in mud, with the uniformity of the material presents an absolutely harmonious aesthetic appearance. At San'a, the stone and bricks which have been widely used particularly in the last two centuries, have created an eclectic and varied style of architecture, the most typical decorative elements being the large multi-coloured windows and rich brick patterns.

As we have said, the architecture of the Tihāma is different from that of the plateau; first of all, it is of a prevalently spontaneous character. The dwelling, usually built of wattle and daub with a single storey above ground level, consists

of several separate rooms in an enclosure in which there are the services and a few shelters for the animals and for the siesta. In the Tihāma north of Hodeydah the huts are particularly well cared for. The conical roof made of straw and canes is tied down with thick ropes, and the inside of the building is finished with clay plaster of a pale ochre colour. Often simple, tasteful decorations with bright colours, done by the women, cover the walls and ceiling with pictures of utensils, vehicles, animals and plant motifs.

This way of breaking up the plan into different blocks of building can be seen in the big cities as well as isolated dwellings and small villages. At Zabīd the ancient historical and cultural tradition of this great Islamic centre reveals itself architecturally through extremely refined and complex structures yet preserves the layout common to the whole Tihāma area. At Zabīd the use of baked brick and stucco is prevalent. Even the most important houses are rarely two or three storeys high, and even if the decoration confers a rich luxurious aspect on the building, it still maintains a substantially simple character. The Government palace is an exception, but it still belongs to the typically eclectic architecture of the Red Sea coastal areas found again in al Makha', al Luheiyah and old al Hudāydah.

Throughout the Tihāma, on account of the hot humid climate, with its very high temperatures from March to October, the dwellings are built down to the last particular so as to obtain maximum ventilation and the greatest amount of protection from the sun. In old Hodeydah shelters on the terraces, somehow echoing the shelters in the enclosures already mentioned, are common as are the curved wooden sunshades over the windows. The

33. Hodeydah (al Hudāydah), palace near the old port.
34. Mokha (al Makha'), ruins of the old town.
35. Mokha, al Shādhili Mosque.   36, 37. Detail of stucco decoration (Zabīd). ▷

architecture of Hodeydah, like that of old Geddah and Sawakin, displays a clever use of richly carved wood. Mokha is a large town in gradual decay after the decline of the port. In spite of irreparable damage due to lack of maintenance and the slow inexorable action of weathering, its remains are still impressive. Particularly remarkable is the architecture of the 18th century, rich in overseas influence. The most significant monument is the Great Mosque founded in the 15th century, with its richly decorated minaret. Though the closest comparison to Mokha is Zabīd, the architectural differences between the two cities are remarkable. In Mokha the buildings are all carefully plastered, while at Zabīd there is a clear preference for the brick to be left uncovered. At Mokha the architecture is scenographic, and the same taste can be seen in the decoration, which is mainly in stucco, with large patterns. At Zabīd, on the other hand, both in the external decoration, with its ornamental play of brickwork, and in the internal decoration, with stucco, the motifs consist mainly of minute designs, like textile patterns. It has already been observed that the architecture of Hodeydah and Mokha is somewhat eclectic, being partly imported, and different from the rest of the lowland area. The difference is obvious in the building concept: in the two port towns houses are built in a single block, without a surrounding wall, and have a lot of windows, even on the ground floor (the easy importation of iron bars has enabled them to be supplied with the indispensable grill for centuries). On the upper floors impressive carved wood mashrabiyah recall models common to all the coastal areas of the Red Sea, and, of course, to Cairo.

38. Zabīd, Bab al Shabāriq: eastern gate of the city.
39. Zabīd, Bab al Sahām, northern gate of the city.

In the Yemen isolated houses are very rare, and take on the look of fortresses: the layout of the urban settlements was chiefly intended for defence, the most important centres developing in a relatively restricted circular area surrounded by walls. Only in some cases this plan was subject to variations, always on account of a particular characteristic of the terrain (Ta'izz, Hajjah). Smaller townships consist of a mass of houses huddled together with the outer ones lined up to form an impenetrable curtain with their own walls. This type of layout is of course not very flexible, since there is no possibility of enlarging it without knocking down a remarkable number of buildings. This led to the growth of satellite settlements outside the main wall. The small town of 'Amrān is a fine example of this kind.

The city walls are usually in mud (Sa'dah), sometimes reinforced with a stone facing (San'a), with solid towers of semicircular section, and sentry walk. The gates come in an interesting variety of kinds: the opening is always scooped out of the wall mass, but is sometimes preceded by extremely complex defence works. In some cases the gate is protected on both sides by perpendicular extensions of the walls, forming a long access corridor. This kind of gate can be seen in a large number of pre-Islamic settlements such as al-Beidha (Nashq) in the Jawf. For greater efficiency one of the foreparts can be partly set in front of the gate, as in the case of the northern gate of Zabīd (Bab al Sahām). In other cases the gate is defended by two foreparts with towers in staggered positions, which oblige any would-be attacker to approach the gate in a roundabout way and so expose himself to the defences on all sides (Sa'dah, Bab al Yemen and Bab Najrān; Zabīd, Bab al Qala'at; San'a, Bab al Qasr and Bab el Stran).

There are also gates, mainly built in the last hundred years, of a less

elaborate defence system and with a marked scenographic character. They open straight into the walls and are supplied with an inner guardroom and sometimes with rooms on the upper floor. They vary from the very simple ones with an arch in the centre and without any decorative elements (Rada') to those flanked by semicircular towers which have lost any defensive value, but recall the ancient type of gate ('Amrān; Hodeydah; Ta'izz, Bab Musa; Zabīd, Bab al Shabāriq). Others showing the influence of the 19th century Turkish taste, are decorated with neo-classic motifs (Ta'izz, Bab al Kebīr) or a complex composition of various architectural elements, emphasized by the heavy chromatic play of different materials (San'a, Bab al Yemen). Inside the large cities there is almost always a citadel, situated, wherever possible, high up and always on the edge of the town. Among the most important are those of Sa'dah, Hajjah, San'a, Zabīd, Ta'izz, and Rada'. The last may perhaps be considered the finest fortress of the whole Arabian peninsula. The Yemeni citadel has an ancient tradition, evidence of which can be found in many pre-Islamic cities. The isolated fortress, on the other hand, is an imported innovation alien to the purely local architectural tradition and probably dating back to the first Ottoman conquest of the Yemen. The features and position of the many fortresses that guard roads, passes and valleys are determined by two factors: the adoption of heavy firearms and the need of the occupying government to control the country.

Religious architecture in the Yemen is still practically unknown, and forms an as yet unwritten chapter in the history of Islamic art. This problem really applies to the entire Arabian peninsula, which is presented as absolutely void even in the most recent works on Moslem art. But there is no doubt that the Yemen

is the country richest in buildings that are either completely intact or at least preserve much of their original features. The economic boom experienced over the last decades in Saudi Arabia and other states of the Arabian peninsula has unfortunately led to the irreparable loss of major works of architecture and archaeological remains, which have been submerged under an overwhelming wave of modernization. Entire quarters of ancient towns have been wiped out and many religious buildings, dating back to the early years of the hijrah, have been destroyed or largely transformed. The Yemen, on the contrary, unblessed with oil wealth, has at least enjoyed the positive consequence of preserving most of its historical and artistic heritage.

At first sight religious architecture in the Yemen seems to be more homogeneous than the secular. In general it has to be noted that the Muslim temple, having to fulfil very limited needs, is built with an extremely simple plan and lends itself to few variations. The mosque is above all a house of prayer, not a place for the celebration of liturgical rites like a Christian or Buddhist temple. The only time that the prayer loses its individual aspect to become almost the celebration of a rite is on Fridays at mid-day, when the great crowd of worshippers pray all together, facing the principal mihrab where the Imam stands, leading the prayer. So, apart from this common act on Fridays when the building has a focal point, the faithful pray singly, in any part of the mosque, only united by the fact that they all face the same direction (qibla).

In the Yemen the mosques display the same austere simplicity which, as we have seen, is one of the peculiar traits of local architecture: they lack the complex plan, variety of decoration, rich and at times over-elaborate polychrome facing which are so characteristic

40. San'a, Great Mosque: outer wall.
41. San'a, Great Mosque: the courtyard viewed from the south-east.
42. San'a, Great Mosque: bronze Sabaean door relocated on the outer wall close to the main mihrab.

in the architecture of many other countries in the Islamic world. This is what creates the illusory impression of uniformity already underlined. An analysis of various important buildings in the country will show that differences do exist, not only in the building technique but also in the layout and details. Religious buildings are represented mainly by mosques and mausoleums, or tombs of people renowned for their religious piety or their famous good deeds. The mosques, of different size and importance are numerous, whereas the mausoleums as isolated buildings are fairly rare on the plateau which roughly corresponds to the Zaidi area, where the tombs are usually included in the mosque precinct. The most ancient mosques belong to the so-called Kufah type, which has a square courtyard entirely surrounded by flat-roofed galleries, the one towards Mecca being of the greatest depth. This plan, notable examples of which are the Great Mosque of San'a, the Mosque of Al Jianad, the Great Mosque of Shibām Kawkabān, and the Great Mosque of Zabīd, is found especially in the Friday mosques. The Great Mosque of San'a is one of the most ancient monuments not only in the Yemen but in the whole Islamic world. Founded in the early years of the hijrah while Mahommed was still alive, it underwent numerous renovations and restorations in the early centuries without, however, losing much of its original appearance. The perimeter walls are built with large squared blocks of grey stone, each row laid slightly recessed from the lower row: splendid evidence of late Sabaean building technique surviving in early Islamic times. In the building many fragments from monuments of pre-Islamic San'a are reused. One of the most exceptional pieces is the

splendid bronze door with inscription and decorations in relief. The great simplicity of the outside of the Mosque harmonizes with the austere, bare lines of its vast courtyard, where a small square domed construction stands. This qubbah, built in 1600, possibly on a pre-existing building, though of extremely sober lines and decoration is somehow alien to local architecture and quite obviously influenced by the taste of the Ottoman entourage of the Pasha of San'a who had it built.

In the marvellous carved and painted wood ceiling of the mosque, reflecting at least three different periods between the 8th and 11th centuries, the rich decoration seems quite out of keeping with the rest of the building. Yet it is so minute in detail as to be unobtrusive and so not a strident contrast to the overall sobriety of the mosque. There is an endless variety and fantasy in the coffered design and intricately carved beams. In these the abstraction of arabesque is touched upon, but not completely achieved owing to the prevailing naturalistic taste linked to the tradition of Himyari sculpture, exemplified in some of the ancient marble pieces reused in the Mosque. The Mosque of al Janad, near Ta'izz, founded in the ninth year of the hijrah has also preserved its original plan in spite of restorations, reconstructions and enlargements. What is striking in this building is the utter simplicity of line and lack of any decoration whatever. The flat, primitive-style roof, with visible timber structure, in chromatic contrast with the bare white arches below it, is yet in perfect harmony with the sober lines of the Mosque.

In later mosques the courtyard remains but loses its value as centre of the building to become only a secondary part of it, as for example in the Mudhaffariyah at Ta'izz (founded about 1260, but greatly altered since), where the courtyard is in the southern half of

43. San'a, Great Mosque: detail of the eastern gallery, painted and carved coffered ceiling.
44. San'a, Great Mosque: detail of a re-used pre-Islamic column.
45. San'a, Great Mosque: detail of the roofing, close to the main mihrab.

the mosque and seems to function only as a link between the baths and the mosque itself. In later and smaller cases, as in a mosque at Hādda, near San'a, dating back to around 1700, and unfortunately in a bad state of repair, the courtyard is still in the centre of the construction, but on account of its size, which is tiny in comparison with the covered galleries, it can only be considered an illumination well, even though it undeniably recalls the traditional courtyard.

Nearly all the lesser mosques, both on the plateau and in the Tihāma, consist of a rectangular prayer hall with the mihrab on one of the long sides. The hall is reached through a courtyard, sometimes with porticoes, roofing, or even rooms open on one of the sides. The roofs are flat, with visible beams on the plateau and domes in the Tihāma, where brick replaces wood. In the large cities of the Yemen there are mosques consisting of a square room with one or more domes, preceded by a courtyard entered directly from the outside or through the ablution chambers. This type of mosque, very common at San'a, reveals a clearly Ottoman influence. The most ancient buildings, like the Bakiriyah, date back to the early 17th century. The domes usually have a rich stucco decoration in relief also on the outside and are flanked on the four corners by brick pillars, for static as well as for decorative purposes. Minarets are nearly always present in the important mosques, especially in the large plateau cities where, in the context of the imposing secular architecture, they have to reach exceptional heights. The oldest minarets, such as those of the Great Mosque of San'a, dating back to the 13th century at least, are very simple constructions covered with plaster and almost completely undecorated. In the Zaidi area the

49. Mosque at Hadda (San'a), interior.

50. San'a, at Bakiriyah Mosque.
51. San'a, qubbat al Mutawakkil, detail of the dome.

minaret appears after the 3rd century of the hijrah. It takes on a very typical appearance, especially at San'a: on a tall square base two polygonal stumps stand one on the other in decreasing order, with the balcony in between. The decoration on this very simple construction stands out sharply on account of the strong chromatic play of the projecting elements, which are plastered against the background of visible brick. At Ta'izz, on the other hand, another kind of luminous effect prevails achieved by a strong animation of the surfaces through the muqarnas pattern and deep blind arches. Good examples of this style are the two minarets of al Ashrafiyah, the minaret of the mosque of Abd al Hadi and the minaret of the Mudhaffariyah (collapsed in 1962). While the chromatic decoration can be convincingly compared with local motifs (so much so that the decoration of the trunks in many minarets of San'a, if unrolled, can easily be compared with the typical ornamentation on the façades of the houses), the light effect seems to be derived from external models, perhaps to be found in Mamluk Egypt. In the important mosques we have seen that, at least on the plateau, almost all have a minaret except in very few cases: one outstanding example is the 'Amariyah at Rada'. In this lovely, early-16th century mosque displaying influences from Oman and perhaps from India, the minaret is reduced to a domed niche standing in the middle of the façade. The Turkish occupation did not lead to the adoption of the typical Ottoman

52. *View of San'a, with the minaret of Salah al Din Mosque.*
53. *San'a, Talha Mosque.*

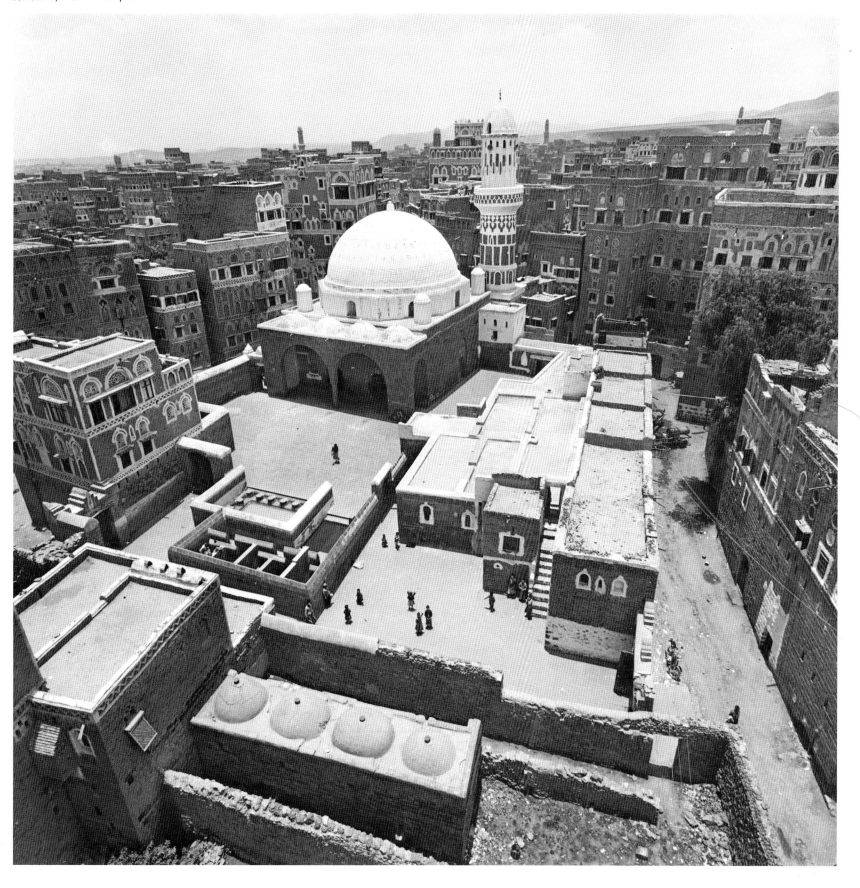

54. San'a, Great Mosque, eastern minaret.
55. Ta'izz, Al Ashrafiyah Mosque.
56. Rada', 'Amariyah Mosque, small minaret in the middle of the south side.

minaret in the Yemen. Even in the Tihāma, in mosques built by the Turkish authorities, the Yemeni taste prevails with extremely simple, sturdy towers, rather squat in form. The only Ottoman-style minaret existing in the whole Yemeni territory is the one belonging to the mosque of the infantry garrison of San'a, which was built during the most recent Turkish domination. In the Ismaili area there are minarets shaped like sugar-loaves, with or without relief decoration depending on whether they are built in stone (Manākha) or brick (Giblah). Another important complement to the mosque is the bathing section for pre-prayer ablutions and the thermal baths which are always associated with the mosque. A good example is the interesting complex of bath and small domed rooms annexed to the mosque of al Jianad, which is supplied by a cistern and by a well set inside the mosque itself. In 1971, together with my colleague Mutahhar al Iriani, I found the remains of a small adjacent thermal bath, buried in the "tell" which had formed all round the mosque. There was no sign of an apodytherium, and it seems certain that there was no frigidarium. The calidarium was a square, dome-covered room, now mostly in ruins. Even though it was impossible to carry out a thorough excavation in this bath, we can safely say that it has ancient characteristics and must date back to pre-Turkish times. It can perhaps be dated to the early 16th century A.D., if identified with the bath a monarch of the Tahirid dynasty (possibly Amer Abd al Wahhab) is supposed to have had built, according to a tradition still upheld by local scholars. The thermal bath is one of the most important elements in Islam. According to many mediaeval writers, who talk of a large number of baths in the city of San'a alone, it was built very early in the Yemen. As no research has yet been carried out in the archives or with

57. Ta'izz, qubbah al Huseyniyah.
58. Al Janad, thermal baths, detail of the calidarium.
59. Al Janad, view of the ablution rooms annexed to the Mosque.

archaeological excavations in connection with this question it is not yet possible to establish how the thermal bath was set out in early Islamic Yemen, or whether we can believe Yemeni historians when they claim its presence even before the advent of Islam. It might well have existed during the Persian domination, as we know of baths in Sasanian Iran. If it were to go back to an earlier period it might be explained either through contacts between Southern Arabia and the Roman world or by the independent development of a local type of bath. The first hypothesis seems the more likely, yet the second cannot be entirely ruled out considering how important ablutions were in pre-Islamic religion and the value of purification Moslems attach to washing in thermal baths, which in Islamic cities are always associated with mosques. As we have said, the isolated mausoleum is more common in the Tihāma and in the southern part of the country, a territory corresponding more or less to the Shafa'i zone. A fine example of this kind of monument is the Huseyniyah, a domed tomb inside the walls of Ta'izz, near Bab Musa. It consists of two parts, belonging to widely differing periods: a solid octagonal structure in ashlar masonry and a plastered brick dome. The interior is decorated with stucco and monochrome paintings with plant motifs and reveals at least two distinct periods, forming one of the most important examples of Islamic decoration in the Yemen. The madrasah (Koranic school) is not very common as a separate building in the Yemen, as religion is chiefly taught in the mosque itself. There are a few exceptions, as for example, a fine group of buildings at Thila' including the prayer hall/madrasah, a large bath and the students' rooms, but normally the madrasah is represented by premises closely connected with the mosque, and with students' rooms also within the main building.

SA'DAH

Sa'dah is the only large city in the Yemen that has so far managed to remain completely uncontaminated by modern development. The surprisingly harmonious architectural unity of its buildings gives it an unreal, ageless appearance. The mud wall encircling it is like a gigantic ribbon, which has drawn within it scattered houses and left the surrounding plain bare and empty. Standing out against the dark background of the mountains the ochre-coloured walls with the sparkling white tops of the houses make Sa'dah look like something out of a fairy tale book. The city is situated to the extreme north of modern Yemen and for centuries has been the political and commercial centre of a vast area stretching from the Red Sea to the Rub' al Khali. Its importance is due to its key position between the great wadis that rise in Hadhramut and the central tableland. For centuries it has been one of the main points on one of the major commercial and pilgrim routes along the peninsula. No traces of pre-Islamic times have been found as yet, but there are numerous Sabaean inscriptions in rock tombs and remains of ancient habitations in the neighbourhood of the city. With the spread of Islam Sa'dah became particularly important when, at the end of the 9th century, Yahya Ibn Huseyn al Rassi, the first Imam of the Zaidi dynasty, established his residence there. A week's caravan journey away from San'a, situated in the middle of a mountainous, semi-desert area, Sa'dah was for centuries the inaccessible refuge of the Imams, who withdrew there in difficult times, during struggles with other dynasties and the resistance to Turkish domination. There are no really outstanding buildings at Sa'dah, but the whole town is most attractive to visitors because of its exceptional unity of tone. Partly because it has remained so isolated, Sa'dah has not expanded beyond its walls, unlike other major towns in the Yemen, and has developed in a disorganised fashion, easily contained within the walls, the only fixed points being a huge area kept free of buildings as commercial and

60. Detail of iron-studded door (Sa'dah).
61, 62. Sa'dah, the city and surrounding area seen from the west. ▷

63. Sa'dah, northern gate: Bab Najrān.
64. Sa'dah, market square and Government Palace.
65. Sa'dah, fort, within the town wall.

67. Sa'dah, part of the suq, with large houses in the background.
68. Sa'dah, the gate to the Jewish quarter within the walls.

69. Sa'dah, street in the Jewish quarter. ▷
70. Sa'dah, Jewish quarter, internal decoration of a ruined house. ▷
71. Sa'dah, cluster of houses outside the walls. ▷

administrative centre, and the three gateways, the only means of access to the town, which are closed at sunset even now. The vast great irregular central square is dominated by the Government Palace and by an impressive fortress standing on a hill, the only elevated part of the city, probably the site of an ancient citadel.

On examining the town one notices huge areas without buildings. They are partly due to the necessity to protect land areas for growing crops, but mainly to provide space for large caravans. In the urban development of Sa'dah these areas have represented a safety valve. The town wall encircles an area of about three square kilometres occupied by a relatively small number of houses, which explains the lack of external expansion. The Jewish community has also remained within the walled area, in contrast to other towns in the Yemen inhabited by Jews, where the alien community has been relegated outside the walls probably on account of shortage of space when there was a spurt of urban development or sudden growth in the population.

The Jewish quarter is surrounded by walls and has two gates. The streets are very narrow and the houses are small but well built. As we have already seen, Jewish houses are usually very sober on the outside, owing to the strict laws imposed by the Imams, but they are carefully decorated inside. Sa'dah is particularly rich in this.

Monumental and naïf, impressive in size but at the same time extremely simple in decoration and detail, the architecture of Sa'dah is without doubt the most surprising manifestation of building technique in the Yemen. Even the most important buildings, at times so impressive as to evoke the fairy tale descriptions of the Himyari palaces, are extremely simple in layout, access and decoration. Together with the general features, the building material itself

72. Sa'dah, zabūr courses at different stages of drying out during building.

73. Sa'dah, detail of a wall: stone foundations with uncoated zabūr courses.

contributes to the aesthetic appearance of the buildings. These are made with squared stones and a clay mortar. The perimeter foundations stand only slightly above ground level, but are gradually raised to a metre at the corners, where they form a sort of "keystone" for the clay strips. Each layer of clay spread out to an even height of about 60 centimetres, is beaten with large wooden spatulas and dries on the spot.

This building technique gives the house a most particular plastic value making it very different from a construction built with blocks, whether they are of stone or sun dried brick. In fact, unlike the stone blocks or unbaked bricks that make up a squared form, the pisé, or "zabūr" (as it is called in the Yemen) forms a modelled construction, with rounded corners and volumes tapering upwards. The houses seem to have grown naturally out of the earth, and retain the same colour. The rows of pisé, almost like the growth rings on a huge tree, form a continuous body in which doors and windows seem to have been cut out at a second stage. Often the building is plastered over, and the rows of pisé hidden under a thick layer of clay. The monument-like appearance of even the smallest buildings is chiefly due to the lack of windows on the lower floors and to the tapering of the construction. The only exceptions to this technique are in the three city gates and in the main religious buildings. The sides of Bab Najrān, for example, are made of large uneven stones carefully dressed in drywall construction, the only decorative note being the external edges of the jambs which are highlighted by a shallow, sharp indentation finishing just below the architrave with a very simple pendent. The al Nizāri mosque, one of the most important in the city, is built with blocks of squared stone in the lower part of the walls and baked bricks in the upper part and crown. The same technique can be seen again in the Great Mosque, containing the tomb of the Imam Yahya Ibn Huseyn. In the plan and distributive elements the houses of Sa'dah, apart from the ones in the Jewish quarter, do not differ from the general type on the Yemenite plateau. Here

74. Sa'dah, house; in the foreground, a small cistern with ablution troughs.
75. Sa'dah, group of houses; in the foreground a clay pit.

76. Sa'dah, house.
77. Sa'dah, glimpse of the town.

78. Sa'dah, Bab Najrān, detail of the stone jambs.
79. Sa'dah, al Nizāri Mosque.
80, 81. Sa'dah, large palaces close to the town wall. ▷

82. Sa'dah, large house.
83. Sa'dah, door of recent construction.

84. Sa'dah, ancient door, detail of architrave with inscriptions. ▷

85. Sa'dah, detail of door with ornate knocker. ▷

again there are no inner courtyards, but it should be observed that the building is sometimes surrounded by an encircling wall to create a closed space of varying size on the four sides. The ground and second floor are used for stables and storehouses for grain and firewood; the third floor for the kitchen, women's and children's rooms and baths. Higher up are one or more floors with bedrooms and baths according to the size of the family, then a spacious belvedere for meetings, the afternoon siesta and receiving guests. This is the only room which reflects its important function with a certain wealth of decoration, both externally and internally. The windows, closed with carved, wooden shutters often have several orders of openings with alabaster panes. This series of openings lets a glimmer of light filter through, the only natural light to penetrate the room when the shutters are closed. The openings are framed on the outside with simple chalk mouldings and form a motif which, with the elements repeated in decreasing size upwards, helps to give the building the soaring appearance already created by its tapered shape. There are only a few examples of the large windows with stained-glass lunettes which are characteristic of San'a architecture. Another important decorative element in the architecture of Sa'dah is the carved wood: great care is given to the doors, where the rich archaic-looking ironwork matches the carvings. The architraves usually have elaborate religious writings on them, sometimes dated and inserted in a rich sophisticated composition of decorative motifs. This taste for wood, partly due to the intrinsic worth of the material, which has to be imported, is widespread enough to have simpler, though just as attractive versions. Treatment to doors and windows is always a refined, sophisticated accessory. One feels that as a material, wood is basically alien to the genuinely local architecture: the pisé, the poorest of materials, which is in fact simply mud, is the great means of expression of Sa'dah builders. With it they have been able to create real works of art halfway between

architecture and sculpture.
The walls of Sa'dah are the pisé structure least contaminated by other materials, and local building seems to have found here its most genuine expression. Bab Najrān is without doubt the most attractive point, and it is in my experience the finest piece of architecture ever produced using pisé. The walls straighten out and curve like a plastic mass to form the forestructure of the gate, in a dynamic and powerful design, concluded by the front tower. This is modelled in a cubist-style anthropomorphous shape that seems surprisingly appropriate to its function as a watch-tower. Outside the walls the plain lies bare and dotted with blackish patches formed by huge slag heaps; a group of unusual tombs appears unreal in the dusky light of sunset.

MANĀKHA

Standing 2500 metres above sea level, on a high mountain pass, overlooked by Jabal Shibām and the massif of Jabal Haraz, Manākha is a typical example of stone-built architecture. Perhaps on account of its high position, though dominated by even higher mountains, it is unlike any other town in the Yemen, and has a special atmosphere of its own. Hajjah, for example, though similar in its architecture, has a different character, for it stands out dramatically against the surrounding mountains.

Manākha, on the other hand, does not lie on the mountain but in it. It belongs to the mountain and has retained the same rugged look and colour. If it were not for the white edging around the windows, the houses would be indistinguishable from their rocky foundation, and easily confused with the mass of rubble and discarded stones around them.

The roughly squared blocks often give a rustic look to the drystone, strongly tapered walls. In the oldest houses windows are few and small. There are hardly any embrasures on the lower floors, and owing to the steep slope of the ground, the downhill side of the building is largely a solid mass of wall. On the upper floors the rectangular, shuttered windows seem quite small in comparison with the lunettes with their panes of alabaster. The light they allow through is in fact less then would appear at first sight, owing to the presence of a second, internal slightly recessed stone frame. Usually there is a ventilation window between the two lunettes. Shade-hoods and other wooden accessories are only used to a very limited extent.

In the centre of a huge terraced area, which is cultivated right up to the most impassable peaks, the town of Manākha also stand on terraces, the result being an enormous amphitheatre of houses with the auditorium furrowed here and there by rough stone flights of steps. The houses are huddled together in the centre, and in the suq the narrow alleys, flanked by shops on either side, wind tortuously along, full of twisting side passages, covered passages and sudden turns. The mass of Jabal Haraz,

dominating Manākha towards the southwest, was the home of the Ismailite sect and birthplace of the Suleihid dynasty, which in the 11th century conquered the Yemen right down to the shores of the Indian Ocean. Nowadays there is no Ismailite colony in the city, but there are many in neighbouring villages and in the Haraz area. It is the goal of pilgrimages from religious centres all over Islam and especially from India.

The mosques of Manākha are extremely simple, with sugarloaf minarets, typical of Ismailite areas. In this small mosque on the eastern slope of the city the minaret looks like an obelisk, hardly interrupted by the design of the balcony: a timid allusion to the building's real function. The fusion of mosque and minaret is interesting, the various elements coming close together without joining, almost like movable blocks. The rough white decoration of the trunk, produced by inserting limestone blocks between the basalt, is as fascinating as a design woven into woollen matting.

Manākha stands most probably on the site of an ancient settlement, but no traces have yet been found of it. The town became important after the first Turkish domination, when it was turned into a fortified centre on one of the main routes between the coast and San'a. The ancient road climbed up from Hodeydah to Manākha, touching the villages of Marawa and Hugeilah. In this stretch the modern asphalted road takes a completely different route, but in the stretch between Manākha and San'a the ancient mule-track is still visible in many places, wide and well built, with sturdy support walls. This century, prior to the construction of the present road, which was completed about ten years ago, the link between Hodeydah and San'a was provided by another road. It climbed up along inner valleys as far as Ma'bar on the Ta'izz-San'a route, crossing the large villages of Madinat al Abid and Hammam Ali. The opening of this road was welcomed by Imam Yahya, as he liked to frequent the thermal bath of Hammam Ali, but it reduced the importance of the old road, which could only be driven along for a

88. Detail of a stone wall (Manākha).
89. Manākha, view of the town towards Jabal Shibām. ▷
90, 91. Manākha, glimpses of the town. ▷

92. Manākha, street in the suq.
93. Manākha, glimpse of the town: a water tank.

94, 95. Manākha, mosque on the eastern slopes of the town. ▷

96. Manākha, beginning of the town and the last terraces on the western slope; large cisterns are also visible.

97. Manākha, part of the western slope of the town; the clashing intrusion of recent architecture is quite visible.

100. Manākha, glimpse of the town.

third of the distance, and consequently of Manākha as a fortified pass. Manākha is only a few minutes' drive from the main road. Where the approach road branches off, a small cluster of houses is rapidly developing as a stopping and refuelling place. Its relative isolation may perhaps help to lessen the damage wreaked on Manākha by sudden, hasty, modernization and may give the inhabitants and authorities time to realise the need to plan its inevitable modern development in harmony with the use of local materials and the traditional ways of building. The recent, mistaken insertion of alien architecture, an intrusion of a yet unspoilt environment, has at least shown up the value of solutions that can be adopted by local builders, independent of external influences and respectful of local tradition, so as to achieve the kind of architecture suitable for changed living requirements. An interesting example of valid building is seen in the partial reconstruction and expansion of the town, carried out at the turn of the century on a small hill, where a group of sturdy houses, with plenty of window space have been built. They are modern yet perfectly in keeping with the general atmosphere and the older houses. The charm of Manākha certainly is in its position, in its magnificient views, and unexpected glimpses of majestic scenery, but I think the real reason for the strong impression it makes on the visitor is the wise and at the same time primordial use of stone, which, takes pride of place in this exceptional city. The stone, cut in squared blocks and uneven pieces, becomes a soft mantle of wide, flowing surfaces spreading out at varying heights along the slopes of the terraces.

On spacious wall surfaces, almost without openings, the decorations are stones and joints, and nothing else. It is an architecture that gives the impression of enormous, brutal strength due less to technique than to the impenetrable nature of the rock itself.

ZABĪD

In the bare sandy plain of the Tihāma Zabīd signals its approach with isolated white mosques, which increase in number as one nears the city.

Half-way between Hodeydah and Mokha, and about twenty kilometres from the sea, Zabīd is on the edge of a fertile area. Its economy relies on agriculture and religious legacies and its fame on the ancient tradition of theological studies. In almost twelve centuries of history Zabīd has never experienced periods of decline and neglect, unlike the Red Sea ports, with their dependence on the uncertain fortunes of commerce. Founded, or reconstructed and enlarged in the early 9th century, when it became the capital of the Ziyadid kingdom, Zabīd kept its importance for seven centuries, under various dynasties, up to the first Turkish conquest. From then on the city became the military and administrative centre of a fairly limited area, but it seems to have become even more important as a religious centre and seat of Koranic and theological studies of the Shafa'i school. The reputation enjoyed by Zabīd in the Sunnite world ever since the 12th century procured the city an enormous number of donations in money and property linked with mosques and annexed schools for religious instruction (madrasah). Over eighty of these madrasah-mosques still survive to prove the importance of Zabīd as a cultural centre, which has only begun a slow decline in the last few years.

To ensure a possible reflourishing of studies, intended in the sense of modern scientific research, there are still many libraries at Zabīd, kept in mosques or madrasah or private property belonging to families descending from famous theologians and scholars.

As we have already seen, many of the mosques of Zabīd are to be found outside the town, striking an odd note in a countryside where isolated buildings do not normally exist. They are very simple buildings, mostly consisting of a hall with one or more domes, preceded by a courtyard around which there are rooms open on one of the long sides. These mosques usually contain the tomb of

101. Detail of stucco decoration (Zabīd).
102. The environment of Zabīd. ▷

103. Zabīd, Mustafa Pasha Mosque outside the town wall. In the foreground, the dome of the mosque in the citadel (al Iskanderiyah).

104. Zabīd, al Kamalīyah Mosque outside the south gate of the city.

105. Zabīd, view of the town from the south. ▷

106. Zabīd, group of houses.
107. Zabīd, parts of a house: façade of the main block.

108. *Zabīd, glimpse of the town.*

109. *Zabīd, doorway to the Government Palace.*

110. *Zabīd, al Asha'ir Mosque: interior with wooden pulpit.* ▷

111. *Zabīd, al Asha'ir Mosque: minaret.* ▷

112. Zabid, Great Mosque: view of the wing reserved for the Koranic school.

the donor to whom they are dedicated, and are surrounded by small cemeteries. The presence of a well or cistern for ablution means that the surrounding land can also be effectively irrigated, appearing as lush vegetation in dramatic contrast with the sandy terrain and the white mosques. The built-up area of Zabīd developed quite spontaneously inside the irregularly circular town walls with its four gates. Towards the east the wall incorporates a great fortress with two gates, one towards the outside, now walled up, and one leading into the city. The walls of Zabīd probably date back to the 9th century A.D. when the city assumed the role of capital of the Banu Ziyad kingdom. The empty spaces in modern Zabīd can be explained either by the fact that the area defined by the walls provided more space than eventually proved necessary for the growth of the city or by the later destruction of buildings. It is interesting to note that as far back as 1763, Niebuhr found the walls knocked down and reduced to a gigantic ring of tell, inside which the town had many empty spaces. Apart from the vast square facing the entrance to the castle, which was probably a respected area right from the early days of the settlement, in other empty spaces the uneven ground and the presence of rubble on the surface proves that buildings once stood there.

As we have seen, the houses are composed of various isolated buildings within a walled, partly cultivated area. Among the various units a main building stands out more richly decorated than the rest and is usually whitewashed. It is rectangular in plan, with access on one of the long sides, and has more or less the same function as the māfrej on the plateau. The typical decoration of architecture of the Tihāma reaches its highest level at Zabīd. The façades of the most important buildings are divided into panels bearing various ornamental motifs carried out with the use of projecting bricks. It is a technique which is very similar to that found at San'a, but with an important aesthetic difference: at San'a the decoration follows a taste for design, and only the projecting parts are whitewashed, at Zabīd the façades are monochrome with the bricks either visible or completely whitewashed, and the decoration consists of a play of chiaroscuro.

Leaving the bricks visible is a simple but extremely attractive characteristic of this kind of architecture. The walls take on a soft and pleasing look, partly because the individual bricks stand out clearly on the surface, which has been worn down by the continual action of wind and sand. In contrast with the extreme simplicity of these walls, the surfaces with a stucco finish stand out even more strongly on account of the lavish relief decoration and carving, which is sometimes of oriental, especially Indian, inspiration. Stucco is used mainly for the decoration of the inside walls. On the outside, apart from the ornamentation above the doors, a particularly interesting element is the stucco grills on the windows. These can be compared with the stained-glass lunettes of San'a which in their turn can be considered variations of lattice lunettes. Both solutions are obviously influenced by climatic conditions. Religious architecture in Zabīd acquires its attractive look from extreme simplicity. The beauty of buildings like the al Asha'ir Mosque or the Great Mosque is certainly not in decoration.

114. *Zabīd, part of the citadel and entrance gate to the town.*

115. *Zabīd, northern part of the citadel and al Iskanderiyah Mosque.*

116. *Zabīd, citadel: part of the walls seen from the east.* ▷

117. *Zabīd, citadel: detail of the walls and base of the minaret of al Iskanderiyah Mosque.* ▷

118. Zabīd, the citadel from the south-east.
119. Zabīd, the citadel from the north-east.

A succession of pointed arches set directly on thick columns without bases or capitals creates the purest division of space outlined by the light reflected by the intradoses. The austere surrounding makes rich pieces of furniture or decoration stand out even more strongly. In the al Asha'ir Mosque there is a precious carved minbar, dating back to the 12th century: a piece of exceptional interest, because used exclusively for reading and commenting the Hadith (Tradition of the Prophet) and not for the khutbah (Friday sermon), which is read from another minbar. The same mosque has a minaret, with a curious "meshwork" decoration and surmounted by a muqarnas cupola (honeycomb-dome) a feature imported from the Syro-Mesopotamian world. One of the pictures of the inside of the Great Mosque shows one of the mosque's main functions. Besides being a prayer-hall, the mosque is also a religious school, but most important for general education: male illiteracy, in fact, is quite negligible in the Yemen. The main characteristic of the architecture of Zabīd is the contrast between the dainty decorative details and the clear-cut, lines of the building: the continuous vibration of the ornate surfaces and the curtain of the walls interrupted only by the structural articulations.
Leaving Zabīd one feels that the minute details lose their consistence and value. What remains is the strong impression created by the basic simplicity of the architecture, which seems best expressed in the plastic mass of the powerful walls of the fortress.

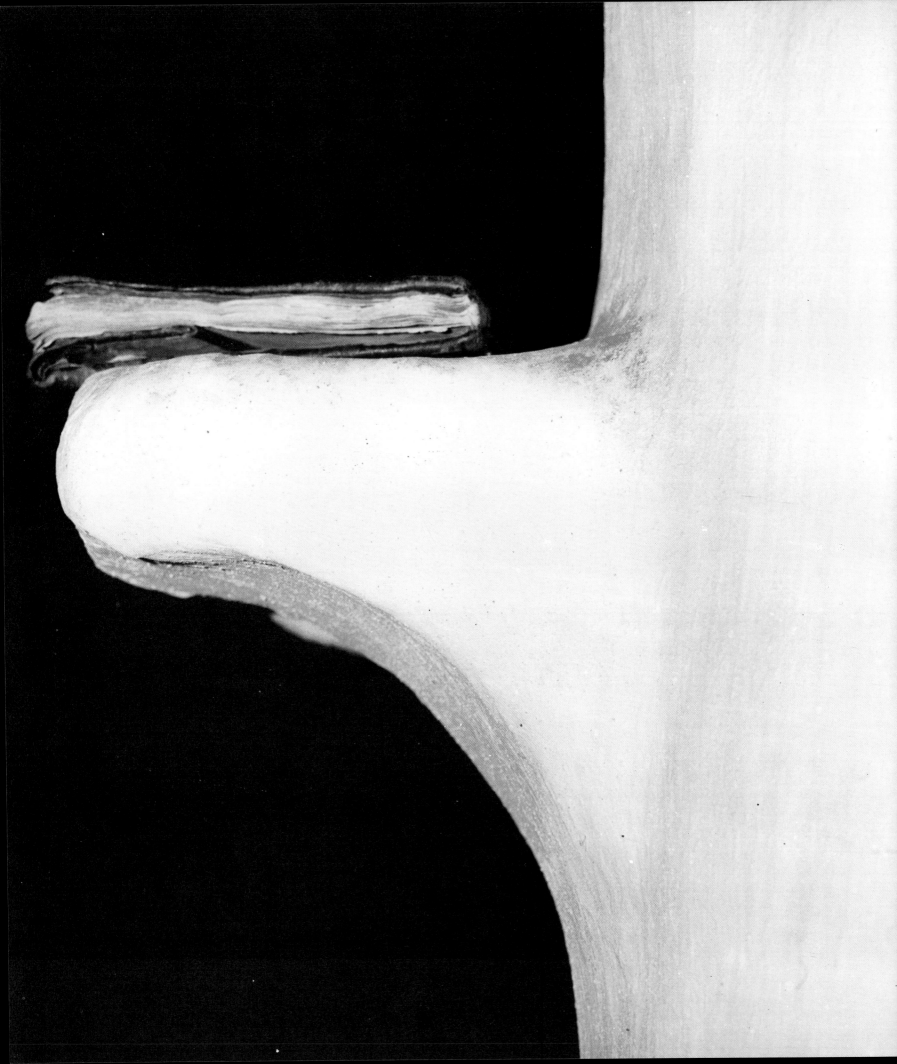

SAN'A

If the Yemeni civilization is reflected mainly by its architecture, the unique town of old San'a is without doubt its most outstanding monument. Its quarters, mosques, gardens, palaces and markets constitute an almost unspoilt environment with few rivals elsewhere in the world. In San'a we find all the forms of building that we have seen adopted in other parts of the Yemen, but the city has its own unmistakable character. The external walls of the houses are richly decorated with patterns that spread over them as over a sheet of paper or a screen. It is an aggressive decoration, accentuated by the whitewash, which makes the linear motifs stand out distinctly against the walls of visible brick, which also become an integrating part of the decoration; brief pauses which rhyme and scan the whole.

As we have seen in the architecture of the plateau, the inner decoration is given more importance than the outer. Instead of the architecture of volumes like that of Thila', Shahāra, Ibb and Sa'dah, at San'a a taste for façade decoration prevails, most probably a fashion of the last two hundred years. The oldest houses can be distinguished by archaic, round openings with alabaster panes above relatively small windows which have shutters with a smaller opening in each panel, typical of the period prior to the introduction of glass. In the decoration of the façade mainly produced by a play of projecting bricks, geometric and symbolic motifs are mingled with stylized floral designs. In these houses, windows play a minor role, being mere openings in the mesh of the decorative design.

In more recent buildings the decoration responds more definitely to a taste for design and is largely whitewashed. The windows play a dominant role with the strong decorative effect of the stained-glass lunettes. In the most ancient examples the façade decoration is a mere surface device and has no direct relationship with the structure and plan of the building. We are tempted to define these façades as scenographic backgrounds superimposed

120. Shelf with Koran (Great Mosque, San'a).
121. San'a, typical architectonic decoration.

on the severe traditional architecture. The original structure remains visible in the lower part of the house, giving it an even severer, bare look in contrast to the festive decoration on the upper floors.

Niebuhr, who spent a week at San'a in 1973, observes: "I think I only saw glass in the windows of one building near the castle (Qasr). The other houses only have shutters on the windows, that are left open in good weather but closed when it rains". Stained glass must have been a novelty of the age, for later on Niebuhr says: "Arabs of a higher social level have coloured glass imported from Venice in their country houses". As regards the materials used in building, Niebuhr observes that while the great palaces are constructed in stone and burnt bricks, most of the houses of San'a are in unbaked brick. The Danish explorer's account of his journey gives us a precious insight into what San'a must have looked like in the second half of the 18th century. On one side he confirms the relative chronology of the architecture based purely on a stylistic analysis, on the other he makes it possible to give a date to the great stylistic innovation that has given San'a its typical look.

San'a stands at a height of 2400 metres in the centre of the Yemen plateau, on the eastern side of a long narrow plain, surrounded by high barren mountains. The Jabal Nuqum, crowned by a triangular fortress, dominates the old town, while the western side of the city, Bir al Azab, stretches fanwise into the countryside. Even though San'a has not always been the capital of the Yemen during its history, it has for centuries been the symbol of the country, and its centre not only geografically, but also from a spiritual point of view. In modern times, ever since Vasco da Gama's travels signalled the beginning of European commercial expansion towards the East, contacts between the Yemen and the outside world became more and more frequent, but until recently foreigners got no further than the commercial centres along the coast, Luheiyah, Hodeydah, Mokha. To these travellers and merchants San'a, a week's hard journey away among impassable mountains, seemed to be the symbol of an unknown country, a holy, forbidden city, the home of the Imam. It was the city that had to be reached if one was really to know the Yemen.

Until a few decades ago San'a was completely encircled by its walls, apart from a nucleus of military barracks built during the last Turkish occupation to the south of the walls, and a small settlement dating back to early Islamic times which developed outside Bab al Sha'ub, around the tomb of one of the Prophet's companions, Farwah Bin Museik.

Since the civil war that followed the revolution in 1962 San'a has again taken over the role of capital, which in 1948 had passed to Ta'izz, and on account of the new government's political openness it has become the headquarters of many foreign embassies. In this way the city has acquired an international tone, but although the capital of a modern state, it still keeps many backward infrastructures. This co-existence of new and old is in fact one of the most surprising aspects of San'a, which has maintained a pleasant rhythm of life and is still on a human scale.

The most attractive point of San'a is without doubt the sailah (seasonal river-bed). This potential river looks like a curious puzzle. The deeply cut bed and meandering course give it the appearance of a river, but water only flows or stands in it for a few days a year. The great stone bridge also makes it look like a watercourse, but as it is traffic that flows through it most of the time, the sailah at this point is more like a modern multi-level road junction than a river.

The beauty of the sailah is mainly of an architectural nature endowed by the scenic way the houses flank it, especially on the eastern bank where they crowd together to form an unbroken front. The wide band of the sailah cuts cleanly through the town from south to north, playing an aesthetic role analogous to that of the town wall: the sailah in a negative way (ditch being the opposite of construction) leaves the

124. San'a, view of the sailah with the Mahdi Abbas
Mosque and bridge in the background.
125. San'a, houses along the east bank of the sailah.

126. San'a, old city: view of the town from the
sentry-walk of the town wall (south side). ▷

front of the built-up area completely visible; the town wall in a positive way (wall being the essence of construction) constitutes a planned limit to the town, closing in the built-up area and checking its expansion. It is worth mentioning that the great monumental value of the walls of San'a, poor as they are in themselves, lies in their significance in relation to the development of the town. While inside the city the scene is broken up into a thousand different views, along the banks of the sailah one has a sweeping view of houses of all styles and ages.
From the sentry walk along the wall the scene changes again, to become majestic in its grandeur. The great mass of tall houses stretches as far as the eye can see, dotted with even taller minarets, soaring upwards in order to stand out above the impressive mass of construction all round them.
From the top of one of these minarets the flat roofs stand out leaving each building clearly perceptible.
Windows with stained-glass lunettes, the leit-motiv of San'a, are distinctive against the mass of the buildings. They are formed of gypsum panels, about three centimetres thick, left to mature for a few hours on a board, then cut through according to a design with which the craftsmen reproduce impromptu geometric or floral motifs or calligraphy of their own personal repertoire without the help of a cartoon. The slender tracery windows that result are then closed with glass cut to follow the design. In the most important rooms of the richest houses the lunettes have a double panel each with a different design. These multi-colour lunettes have a double effect: on the inside they are vividly coloured with the light filtering through them, while on the outside they are decorative with the bright stucco tracery standing out against the leaden background of the glass. In houses where the design and workmanship of the windows is of a particularly high standard, they are often the only decoration, together with the mouldings that traditionally mark the floors. The few vertical motifs are generally the frames of small windows.

130

Other motifs, which are merely decorative and not related to the tectonic of the building are floral, symbolic or even architectural such as domes and minarets. But this is not the place to list the countless decorative motifs to be found in San'a and, in any case, a study of that kind would become an end in itself, bereft of any real meaning as far as understanding the architecture is concerned. And the architecture of the Yemen is in general so free and spontaneous in its details and decoration that it would be impossible to make a systematic study of it. One would have to write an endless list of items, each different from the other, and be forced to conclude that if a canon does exist it is in the absolute rejection of rules. In San'a even the simplest buildings show signs of a vivid imagination in the choice of often unusual decoration. A large stone and baked brick building, a semsarah of exceptional proportions in the centre of the suq, has its façade divided in the guise of a loggia and from each arch lozange patterns hang like carpets from imaginary parapets. Real architectural curiosities are not infrequent. One house near Bab al Yemen contains all the usual features including a terrace, but is built on a triangular plan; an original and most attractive concept, worthy of a Yemeni Antonelli. As regards decorative curiosities, a good example is the "Palazzo Zuccari" of San'a with smoke outlets shaped like human faces; the first with its mouth half open and the second shouting.

The importance of the reception rooms is shown by the rich decoration on the outside walls. Inside the māfrej is a spacious, well-lit room, both simple and comfortable and the rustic ceiling contrasts sharply with the refined carving of the shelf corbels. In the neat, white architecture of the room the only colour is in the lunettes, cushions and floor mattresses, covered with rugs and carpets of various origin. There is often a picturesque mixture of ancient Persian carpets, Bedouin rugs and recently imported linoleum.

The western part of San'a still keeps its original character of a garden city

131. San'a, house close to Bab al Yemen.
132. San'a, old city: detail of a façade.

133. San'a, view of the old city towards the south-east.

134. San'a, exterior of a māfrej of a large house in the old city (Bait al Watāri).

135. San'a, exterior of Imam Yahya's office in the Mutawakkil.

136. San'a, māfrej of a large house in the old city (Bait al Watāri).

137. San'a, Bir al Azab: part of the town. In the centre, the palace of Prince Ahmed (later Imam), now Ministry of Justice.

138. San'a, view of the sailah and southern khanādiq; in the background, residential quarter of the old city.

139. San'a, Great Mosque: galleries on the north side.

and can be immediately distinguished from the old town by its large green spaces and the low suburban-type houses, interspersed with a few multi-storey blocks which look even more impressive in comparison. The large amount of land available has made it possible in the last few years to build ministries, government palaces and residential quarters in blocks that often incorporate the old country houses. The real, living centre of the city remains the old town of San'a, with its ancient mosques and its markets. These are still divided up according to the various crafts and trades and are regulated by laws which have been in force for centuries; they continue to be a place for exchanging news and information as well as goods, a meeting place for the men of the tribes, merchants, craftsmen and, nowadays, also for foreigners. The suq is above all a man's word: women are excluded by time-honoured tradition, connected with the division of duties within the family life and the tribal organization. The only outside activity left to the woman is the selling of bread and the small commerce of farm and home produce: eggs, poultry, vegetables and baskets.

From dawn to sunset prayers punctuate the day. "Come to the best work of all" add the Zeidis when they make the traditional call, as if to underline the passage from work to reflection. The mosque, the hub around which all Moslem society revolves, has maintained its ancient social and cultural value intact. Apart from being the place where prayers are recited it is the centre of religious culture, elementary instruction, study and meditation. The Great Mosque of San'a stands on the edge of the suq, and is intimately connected with it. Their very closeness stresses the contrast between the crowded, noisy, smelly streets and the calm, silent atmosphere of the mosque. The succession of transverse aisles dividing up the light entering from the courtyard, the closely set pillars, and the proportions of the various elements of the building create

140. San'a, old city: glimpse of a street in the suq.

141. San'a, Great Mosque: the south-east courtyard.
On the right, façade of the library built by Imam Yahya.
142. San'a, Talha Mosque: detail of the dome
and minaret.

143. San'a, view of the mosque and the qubbah al
Mutawakkil (from Dar al Shukr).

a particularly suitable atmosphere for prayer and meditation. Of the forty-seven mosques inside the walls of ancient San'a, some date back to Turkish times and reveal the influence of Ottoman architecture: in these cases there is a central space, covered with a dome of monumental proportions unknown to local tradition. In the architectural context of San'a these great domes are completely alien. Significantly the decorative stucco reliefs belonging to local taste are no more than superficial applications, having no tectonic relationship with the building. Apart from the odd exception, all the mosques at San'a are entered from the street by means of a spacious paved courtyard with a stone-arched colonnade. This partly covered vestibule helps to isolate the prayer hall, ensuring its intimacy and seclusion.

The oldest part of San'a has until now barely been touched by modernization, but even that little has opened a large unhealable wound in the most vulnerable part: the delicate junction between the old city and Bir al Azab. Nowadays, alongside the walls and the remains of the historic centre, there is a road flanked by variously coloured cement buildings, a cheap imitation of the most squalid quarters that have risen up on the outskirts of many Middle-Eastern cities. The mosque, built by the Imam Yahya near the 18th century qubbah, the high mud tower the royal palace and Dar al Shukr, now home of the National Museum, have so far remained immune, but have lost much of their value through the radical change in their original surroundings. At least the individual buildings have been saved, and the danger of blind, unconsidered demolition seems to have been averted. Recent regulations issued by the Ministry of Public Works recommend the use of stone and local materials for new constructions. It has been understood that the ancient building tradition of the Yemen is still alive and must be given the opportunity to remain so.

144. San'a, Daud Mosque, in the old city: glimpse of the entrance courtyard.
145. San'a, panorama from the east.

NOTES ON THE URBAN DEVELOPMENT OF SAN'A

In examining the architecture of San'a we have been able to appreciate the relatively good state of preservation of the old town, especially in the areas east of the sailah. Over the centuries they have obviously undergone alterations and renovations, which are difficult to single out today, owing to the continuity of the building technique and the uniformity of materials used. On the other hand, it is this very lack of innovation in technique and taste, as in social and living conditions that has determined the survival of the original town plan, the individual quarters and in general the atmosphere characteristic of old San'a (the same can be said for many other cities in the Yemen). In addition to the examination of architecture in San'a and in the Yemen as a whole, it may be useful to consider how this city developed. I should like to specify that I will limit my study to a superficial analysis of the town, in order to outline the possible phases in its development. Only a deep study, conducted on the basis of historical and epigraphical research, and with the help of soundings, could give really precise information.

Up to the present day the most important milestones in the mapping of San'a have been the charts made by C. Niebuhr in 1763, R. Manzoni in 1879 and C. Rathjens and H. Von Wissmann in 1929. An important addition was the recent aerial photos ordered by the Government of the Yemen Arab Republic for a town-planning project. San'a must certainly be a very ancient city, but there is no evidence to identify it with the city of Uzal, quoted in the Bible (Genesis: X, 27), and feasibly the origin of the Moslem name of Azal. Its existence in the Sabaean-Himyaritic period is proved by a large number of inscriptions referring to it by its Sabaean name, Sanauw. More proof is provided by the large amount of archaeological material found re-used in religious buildings or private houses, or by chance, whenever the remains of a building are uncovered

146. San'a, aerial photo.
147. San'a, Manzoni's map.

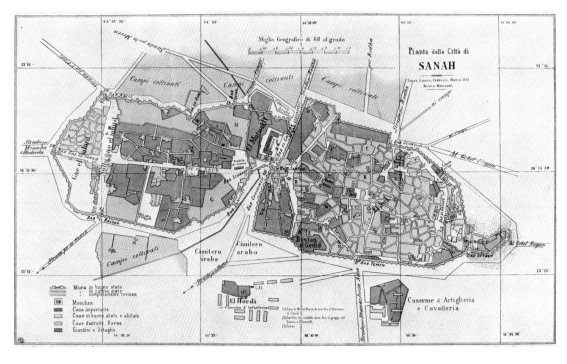

during construction work. Scholars agree that San'a was an important pre-Islamic city, but not about its original role as a caravan city or as a centre of outstanding political-religious character. It can be argued, however, that the pilgrim route to Mecca, which climbs up from Aden and along the plateau, touching San'a, Sa'dah and Najrān follows the ancient commercial and religious route of pre-Islamic times. Mecca was one of the main stopping places, followed by Yathrib (Medina), Khaybar, Dedan (Al 'Ula), Al Higr (Madain Saleh), Teyma, Ma'an and the Mediterranean. One of the most ancient nuclei of the city is probably the Qasr, a century-old fortress, which popular and learned tradition, as well as the name itself (qasr means palace in Arabic) identify as the king's or governor's residence at least in the period immediately prior to Islam. Whatever its original function may have been, and discarding the legend that it stands on the ruins of the famous Ghumdan Palace, the Qasr preserves traces of an ancient constructive phase in its structure, unparalleled so far in San'a, but similar to the remains of ancient Sabaean constructions in the city of Duram (Tayyibah) by the Wadi Dhahr. Presuming that the modern Qasr represent one of the ancient nuclei of the city, we can deduce from its position and from the terrain itself, that it stands on the site of the pre-Islamic citadel, in a town plan analogous, to the one of Ma'rib, Ma'in and Ukhdud (Najrān). The Sabaean nucleus of the city can be hypothetically traced following a circular plan, with its centre between the extreme western limits of the modern suq and the qasr. This centre corresponds more or less to the site called "ghurqat al qallis" (excavation of the church), which must have kept its central position into the late Himyaritic period, but could not have had any important buildings on it, since in 525 it was chosen by Abraha for a Christian cathedral.
With the advent of Islam San'a expanded remarkably in a west-northwest direction. From the aerial photo we can

148. San'a, Great Mosque: re-used pre-Islamic material.

149. San'a, external walls of the citadel, with structures datable to various periods.

150. Tayyibah (Wadi Dhahr), tower and remains of stone structures, probably Sabaean.

trace the possible perimeter of this
stage with a compass centered in the
middle of the modern suq: the extreme
eastern side of the circle touches the
outside of the Qasr, while on the western
side there are some large gardens.
These still keep their juridical status
of religious legacies and their original
purpose as arable spaces found then
at the edge of the town. In this period
of expansion, the Great Mosque was
erected not far from the centre, even if the
large proportions of the building
necessitated the choice of a vacant
piece of land on the edge of the
previously developed area.
As we have seen, the limits of this
expansion skirted the western side of
the modern quarter of the suq, alongside
the Great Mosque. In the early centuries
of Islam, San'a must have expanded
progressively in the same direction,
fanning out to reach the maximum limit
of the sailah, the river bed for the
seasonal waters that flow down from the
mountainous region south-east of San'a
towards the depression formed by the
Wadi Raghwan, 90 kilometres
north-east of the city. The sailah is dry
all the year round apart from a brief
period after the great rains, but even
then the flow of water is very modest.
This is not the place to examine the
climatological problems of the Yemen,
in relation to the possible variations that
have taken place in the last millennia.
We know from historical sources that
in the past many floods caused serious
damage to the city. (During one of them
the Great Mosque is supposed to have
been partly destroyed.) About 1878,
following a heavy flood that made the
sailah impassable, the Turkish governor
of the Yemen built the stone bridge
which is still in existence.
The sailah is therefore a natural form
of drainage that has eroded itself a
meandering bed still intact both inside
and outside the city. There are no traces
of embankments or any attempt to
control the course of the waters for
town-planning purposes, so the sailah
is obviously one of the main factors
conditioning the development of San'a.
It forms a wide ribbon of land,
unsuitable for building, and therefore

151. San'a, old city: cultivated area, site of ancient
clay quarries.
152. San'a, view of the northern khanādiq from
outside. ▷

blocking expansion on the west side
at least for a certain time. As well as
the bridge, there are two other ways
of crossing the sailah where the walls
across the river bed. At this point
there are three arched openings, with
grills in ancient times, to enable the
water to flow through but to ensure
defense.

Another remarkable period of expansion
towards the west and beyond the
bulwark provided by the sailah
probably took place at the beginning of
the Hamdanid dynasty (11th century)
or the Ayyubid conquest of Yemen
(12th century). This extra-mural, or rather
"trans seilam" development, is
represented by the large area of town
between the sailah and the great road
now running parallel to it to the west.
The urban texture of these new quarters,
which were later enclosed in an extension
of the walls, presents very interesting
particulars: first of all there is an oval
"island" in the centre enclosed by two
roads that meet to the west. In this
quarter, known as Nahrein (the two
rivers), the buildings are huddled together
in an irregular mass. South of the
Nahrein there is much more open
space, with large isolated houses
surrounded by gardens and with an
enormous garden on the extreme
southern edge. This is the so-called
Bustan el Sultan (Sultan's Garden)
quarter probably the site of the
residence of the Hamdanid Sultan or
Turan Shah, brother to Sultan Saladin.
North of the Nahrein quarter the
town smooths out into an almost regular
network plan. This quarter seems
relatively recent or was perhaps used
in ancient times for military barracks;
there are however no important buildings
and the constructions are rather low
and simple in appearance.

On the western edge of the Nahrein
quarter stand the group of palaces
belonging to the royal family, known
as the Mutawakkil, and dating back to
the first half of the 18th century at least.
The Mutawakkil includes a mosque,
baths, two palaces, a group of minor
buildings (already used as administrative
offices under the Imam) and a large
garden with a monumental māfrej on

the extreme northern edge.

This group of buildings is enclosed by a wall with a sentry walk even on the side of Bir al Azab, the vast garden city to the west of San'a, which at the time the Mutawakkil was built, in the 18th century, was not yet surrounded by walls. There used to be an inner square between the walls of San'a and the Mutawakkil, forming a kind of parade ground or court of access to the palaces and mosque. But the unfortunate dissection of the town centre, about ten years ago, transformed this interesting point into a simple road, even doing away with the access gates to the square, and destroying its original character.

In Manzoni's map there are four gates: Bab al Shaghadif and Bab Khuzeimah, facing north and south respectively; Bab al Sabah connecting the Mutawakkil with San'a, and Bab Sharara on the western side. Manzoni's documents are the only evidence we have of the town of this period, for afterwards there were alterations that led to the abolition of the eastern gate and reconstruction of the one towards Bir al Azab. This new gate also named Bab al Sabah, consisted of a deep vaulted passage under a low long building of eclectic style with tall rectangular windows, and stone lintels jutting out sharply in the style characteristic of the last Turkish domination. This gate has also disappeared. It was demolished in 1966, during "modernization" work in the centre of San'a. Fortunately we can still see what it looked like in some panoramic photos of the city.

Until the first half of the 19th century the Mutawakkil formed the extreme western limit of expansion of the old city. Hemmed in by its walls, San'a had come to have an oval shape, with the fortified groups of the Qasr and Mutawakkil on either end of the major axis.

Increasing suburban development outside the walls on the western side of San'a, forming the so-called garden, or Turkish city, brought about a gradual shift outwards, along an axis corresponding exactly to the fortified compound of the Mutawakkil, which represents the "seam" joining the two halves of the city. In the absence of any town-planning regulations to protect this group of buildings, the city has been fatally ripped apart.

The western side of the city, or Bir al Azab, as it is commonly called after one of its quarters, included large isolated palaces surrounded by vast cultivated areas, scattered groups of dwellings belonging to peasants, small merchants and craftsmen, and finally the large district formed in the late 17th century to house the Jewish community. In the first half of the 19th century this huge area was surrounded by a wall, smaller than that of ancient San'a and without a sentry walk. It had two gates. Bab al Qaa al Yahud, the gate on the western side, marked the start of the road to Hodeydah. A final interesting phase in the historical development of San'a (the present one does not come into the scope of this work) is represented by the Turkish barracks built between 1871 and 1879 outside the walls, on the southern side of the city. In a certain sense they are repetition of the development extra muros supposed to have taken place in Hamdanid or Ayyubid times. They are two large groups of two-storey buildings, one on the eastern side of the sailah and reached by a bridge. This trapezoidal group of buildings is spread over a large area, and includes a mosque with the only Ottoman-style minaret in the Yemen, as already mentioned. The second group of buildings stands by Bab al Yemen, on the left side of the road to Ta'izz.

It is interesting to note that as a consequence of the building of these barracks Bab al Yemen was also built in a scenographic style unknown to Yemeni taste. The previous gate was like the ones we have seen at Sa'dah and Zabīd, with front towers in staggered position protecting the approach. At San'a the only examples of this type of fortified gate still in existence are the two gates to the Qasr. Bab al Yemen is

153. San'a, al Mutawakkil Mosque. Dar al Shukr is partly visible on the right.

154. San'a, the Turkish barracks with access bridge over the sailah.
155. San'a, Bab al Yemen from outside.
156. San'a, old city: façade of a cistern.

rather squat and clumsy looking. This impression may largely be due to the heavy gable superimposed above the depressed arch, but even in the decoration one senses the stiffness of eclectic inspiration, which has produced a lifeless juxtaposition of motifs. The same taste can be found in a curious fountain (it would be more appropriate to call it a drinking cistern, since the water was kept in a small tank which was periodically filled up. Travellers could get water with a small metal cup attached to a chain). It now stands almost hidden in a blind alley near the Great Mosque, but I have been told that it was transferred there from the Bab al Yemen area. It cannot be called a masterpiece of architecture, but is attractive in its own way. Perhaps it is the broken gable that gives it a certain grace, and the strange decoration on the capitals of the pillars holding up the scalloped arch or the absurd repetition of pillars which fill up the spandrels.

BRIEF HISTORY OF THE YEMEN

The pre-Islamic period

The pre-Islamic civilization of Southern Arabia must be considered in its entirety, without taking into account the political borders of today. Modern Yemen is only a small part of the enormous territory where this civilization flourished: an area extending northwards far beyond Medina, eastwards as far as modern Omān and westwards beyond the Red Sea to include much of modern Ethiopia. Until a few decades ago this civilization seemed to be peripheral and obscure compared to the Mediterranean civilizations, and was studied almost as an exotic curiosity by a handful of specialists. Today it appears intimately connected with the history of the ancient civilization of the Near East, a chapter of the history of the ancient world. One of the main sources of wealth of the Southern Arabian kingdoms was the trading of incense, myrrh and spices brought from India and from Arabia itself to the Mediterranean. Myrrh, and to a lesser extent incense, were used in Egypt from the time of the fourth dynasty, especially for embalming. Later, the demand for incense increased as it came to be used widely in Mesopotamia, Syria, Greece and then in the Roman Empire. Until the 2nd or 3rd century A.D. the trade was mainly by land. The caravans had to pay tolls as they crossed other people's territories, and in exchange were guaranteed safe conduct and provisions. The adoption of the dromedary as a beast of burden speeded up transportation and reduced costs. The endurance and frugality of these animals enabled the caravans to follow more direct routes depending on a smaller number of watering places and control points. The introduction of the dromedary from Asia, and its domestication, has for a long time been seen as a decisive factor in the civilization of Southern Arabia. Until recently, many scholars were agreed in proposing the 10-11th centuries B.C. as the date of the introduction of the dromedary to Arabia, but now it appears that domesticated dromedaries were already in use at least by the middle of the third millenium B.C. Thus the introduction to Arabia of the dromedary as a beast of burden turns out to lose much of its importance, at least in relation to the generally accepted chronology of the Southern Arabian kingdoms.

About the 2nd century A.D. an increasing demand for spices and aromas in the Roman Empire, owing to the spread of oriental cults, encouraged the development of sea transport. Ships of greater size and draught were able to take advantage of the currents associated with the monsoons. The "Periplus of the Eritraean Sea," a book probably written in Alexandria in the 3rd century A.D., describes the sea route between the Mediterranean and India, naming the ports of call and listing the goods exchanged at the various places. Commercial activity provides great stimulus to the growth of civilization, promoting the exchange, not only of goods, but also of ideas, tastes and technology. The "Periplus," if necessary, provides us with evidence of the variety of these exchanges: as regards the port of Muza' on the southern coast of the Yemen for example, the text refers to statues, pottery and works of art imported from the Mediterranean. This information is obviously of great importance as it proves the direct influence of Roman art on that of Southern Arabia.

But, although commerce was one of the chief sources of wealth, it was by no means the only one; we must not forget the flourishing agriculture which made use of sophisticated techniques for terracing, catchment and storage of water, and irrigation: the dam of Ma'rib is the most famous and undoubtedly the most impressive of the numerous hydraulic works of this type constructed in South-Western Arabia. Commerce and agriculture had a marked religious character: borders, canals, water rotas and fields were placed under the protection of the deities, as were spices and aromas, which were gathered to the accompaniment of religious ceremonies.

The Southern Arabian Kingdoms

The chronological scheme of the Southern Arabian kingdoms put forward by Edmund Glaser and based on mediaeval Arab sources, placed the beginning of the Southern Arabian kingdoms with the Minaean one, at the end of the third millenium B.C. This chronology has now been refuted by the majority of scholars and the various kingdoms are no longer seen in succession, but overlapping for a certain period of their history. Two main chronologies have been proposed, based on the study of early inscriptions: one ascribing the most ancient epigraphic documents in existence to the beginning of the 9th century B.C., the other to the 6th century B.C.

Ma'in

The hub of the Minaean kingdom was the Jawf, an extensive plain hemmed in by two ranges of mountains that separate it to the north from the region of Najrān and to the south from the territory of the Arhab and San'a. The capital was Qarnaw, present-day Ma'in, in which the ancient name of the kingdom survives. The city of Ithl (Baraqish) was an important religious centre; its impressive ruins stand a few kilometres south of Ma'in.

The Minaeans played a basic role in the commerce between the Mediterranean and the Dhofār, across the Arabian peninsula. Evidence of their presence in the Mediterranean is provided by a bilingual inscription of the 2nd century B.C. carved on an altar in the temple of Apollo at Delos and by the sarcophagus of a myrrh and incense trader who died in Egypt in 183 B.C. The northernmost Minaean settlement is the city of Dedan (al 'Ula, about 300 kilometres north of Medina).

The fall of the independent Minaean kingdom seems to have coincided with the rise of the Himyarite dynasty in 115 B.C. and Strabo no longer mentions the city of Qarnaw in his account of Aelius Gallus' expedition to Southern Arabia in 24 B.C. But the decline of the Minaeans' political power does not mark the end of their commercial organization. In the north of the peninsula it passed into the hands of the Nabataeans.

Qataban

The kingdom of Qataban had its centre in Wadi Beihan, south-east of Ma'rib and was bordered to the north by the Ramlat as-Sabatayn desert. The capital was Timna (Hajar Kohlan) a rich city, the ruins of which were partly unearthed by an American expedition in 1950-51. The kingdom of Qataban was commercially important owing to its key

position. Even though it apparently never had any outlet into the Indian Ocean, it controlled the Mablaqa pass leading to the sea, and the trade route towards Hadhramut. The wealth of Qataban is proved by the impressive remains not only of the capital, but also of countless hydraulic works still visible today along the Wadi Beihan. The kingdom came to a violent end at the hands of the Hadhramis, who burnt the capital.

The date of this conquest is unfortunately doubtful, and is tentatively attributed to the first quarter of the 1st century A.D. by some scholars, and to the end of the 2nd century A.D. by others.

Awsan

The territory of Awsan lay south of Qataban and extended along the coast, most probably as far as Bab al Mandeb. We have information of a struggle between Awsan and Saba at the end of the 5th century B.C. when the Sabaeans, already in control of the caravan routes, wanted to extend their control to sea trade with the African coasts. The Sabaean king, Kariba'il Watar destroyed and sacked the main cities of Awsan, and took over the coastal area while the inland territory was taken over by Qataban. But as late as seven centuries after these events, in the "Periplus of the Eritraean Sea" there is still mention of the "Awsan coast," indirectly proving how important the kingdom was for overseas trade.

Hadhramut

While commerce was in the hands of Qataban, of the Minaeans and other people west of Wadi Beihan, the most important producer of incense and myrrh was Hadhramut. The political constitution of this kingdom goes back

to the 5th century B.C. The capital was Shabwa, and was mentioned by both Eratosthenes and Pliny, who described it as surrounded by walls and containing sixty temples. The impressive ruins of Shabwa are still visible. It stood in a remote area far away from fertile, cultivated lands, probably in order to control the rich salt mines in the area, and at the same time to provide a collecting and storage point for incense. Brief excavations were carried out in Shabwa in 1938, and more are now being undertaken by a French expedition. From inscriptions we know the names of several kings, and also that one of them conquered Qataban and destroyed Timna. In the latter half of the 3rd century A.D. Hadhramut was conquered and taken over by the Himyarites.

Saba

Saba is the best known of the Southern Arabian kingdoms, partly because its name was favoured by classical writers to indicate the Southern Arabian peoples as a whole. The Sabaean state probably took shape towards the end of the second millenium B.C., in the region between the Rub' al Khali and the territory of San'a. The capital was first Sirwāh in Khawlān and then Ma'rib.

Ma'rib stands on the Wadi Dhana, near the site of the famous dam. The dam was probably already in existence in the 8th century B.C. and was listed in the wonders of the world by mediaeval Arab writers. The Ma'rib dam did not serve as a real reservoir but to distribute the seasonal waters of the wadi over as wide an area as possible. It was made up of an earthen wall covered with squared stones; at each end two sluice gates with openings at different levels diverted the waters into the irrigation channels. All that remains of the dam today are these complicated exit valves. It was restored many times, as is recorded by inscriptions.

In most ancient times the state was governed by priest-kings, the Mukarrib, but in an inscription found at Sirwāh, dating back to the middle of the 5th century B.C., the title of Mukarrib is replaced by that of king. The change of title seems to coincide with a period of territorial expansion, when Ethiopia was also colonised. The kings of Saba were then flanked by a dynasty using the title of "King of Saba and Dhu Raydan." Raydan was presumably the name of a mountain in the territory of Zafār (20 kilometres south-east of Yarīm). Zafār was the capital of this dynasty, which was also identified with the name of the tribe of the Himyarites to which it belonged (the Homeritae of classical writers).

Himyar

The rise of this dynasty is dated to the year 115 B.C., by deducting 525 A.D., year of the Ethiopian invasion, from 640, the date of the same event according to the Himyarite calendar.

The rise of the Himyarites did not cause the fall of the kingdom of Saba, and for a long time the two dynasties shared control of a vast territory stretching from Hadhramut to the coast of the Red Sea, and perhaps including part of Ethiopia as well. About 300 A.D. a Himyarite king united the two kingdoms and took the title of "King of Saba, Dhu Raydan, Hadhramut and Yamanat."

After his death, the Yemen was conquered for a short time by Ethiopian kings, perhaps as a reaction to his expansionist policy.

First Ethiopian Conquest

However brief this Ethiopian domination may have been it had an important consequence, as it introduced Christianity into the country. During this period, in 356 A.D., Constantius Emperor of Byzantium, sent a mission led by Theophilus Indus who seems to have baptised the Himyarite king and been granted permission to build three churches, one of them at Zafār. But at the beginning of the 5th century both king and people seem to have embraced the Jewish faith. The adoption first of Christianity and then of Judaism is proof of the weakening of the traditional religious belief and symptomatic of a deep religious crisis revealed by a tendency towards monotheism, a tendency which largely explains the ease with which Islam was later adopted.
In this period a serious persecution of the Christians broke out, culminating in the notorious massacre of the Christians of Najrān in 523. This offered an official excuse for the return of the Ethiopians, who remained in the country from 525 to about 575 A.D.

Second Ethiopian Conquest

The first Ethiopian governor Abraha chose San'a as his capital, where he built a great cathedral leaving the Bishop's seat at Zafār, where it had been founded towards the end of the 5th century. Abraha also had a church built at Ma'rib and the dam restored.

Sasanian Conquest

The Himyarite nobles asked the Persians to help them drive the Ethiopians out of the Yemen, which had become nothing more than a vassal state of the Ethiopian empire. The Sasanian king, keen in extending his influence beyond the Persian Gulf to the Red Sea, decided to intervene. His army defeated the Ethiopians and the Yemen then became a vassal state of the Persian empire. It was entrusted to a Himyarite king, but on his death passed under the direct rule of the Sasanians and was subsequently governed by five Satraps. During this period of subjection to the Persians, Christians were persecuted. The Yemeni civilization declined, thus creating a political and spiritual void which provided conditions particularly favourable for adoption of the Islamic religion.

From the advent of Islam to the Republic

Already in the very early years after the hijrah, while Mohammed was still alive, there were conversions of the Yemeni tribes to Islam, and in 628 the Persian governor himself, Badhan, embraced the new religion. A real proselytising campaign and political expansion soon followed: a long list of important people, including those closest to the Prophet, such as his son-in-law Ali, were sent to the Yemen in these years, proving how important Mohammed considered this country in the establishment of the new religion in the Peninsula, before considering further expansion.
In the history of the political development of Islamic Yemen, it seems particularly important that in 657 Ali, the fourth Caliph, ordered that the country should have a single governor residing at San'a.

Umayyads and Abbasids

Under the Umayyad caliphs, the Yemen was ruled by governors sent from Damascus. The same system was maintained by the Abbasids, but around the beginning of the 9th century the same thing happened in the Yemen as in many other regions in the vast Islamic empire: the weakening of central power led to the rise of dynasties originating with the governors sent by the caliph, and only nominally subject to the central government.

Ziyadids
In the Tihāma, about 820 the dynasty of the Ziyadids (Banu Ziyad) arose, and the city of Zabīd was chosen as capital.

Ya'furids
From 861 the plateau from Shibām Kawkabān to Al Jianad (Ta'izz) was dominated by the Ya'furid (or Ya'firid) dynasty.

Zaidi Imams
By the end of the century, the people of the plateau north of San'a were ruled by the Zaidi Imams, direct descendants of Ali, with their capital at Sa'dah.
Ali had been assassinated at Kufa in 661. The problem of the succession to the caliphate had caused a schism: Ali's supporters had refused the nomination of Mu'awiyah, as he was not a descendant of the Prophet and had started the Shi'a (literally secession, separation) which was to comprise various sects rejected as heretical by the Sunnites, or orthodox Moslems. Shi'a includes the Zaidi sect which originated and took its name from Ali's great-grandson Zaid, but was built up as a religious doctrine by Qasim bin Ibrahim, called al Rassi after the area where he lived near Medina. According to this doctrine, religious and temporal power has to be represented by an Imam elected from among the Sayyids

(or descendants of Ali's son Huseyn) on the basis of physical and moral qualities of absolute integrity, together with deep theological learning.
This succession of Imams, owing to its religious rather than hereditary nature, has been particularly important in the history of the Yemen from the 9th century to the present day. Following the expansion of the temporal power of the Imams, Zaidi doctrine spread across the plateaux as far as Yarīm and part of the eastern regions, while the rest of the country remained Sunnite after the Shafa'i school.

Qarmathians
In the early years of the 10th century the Qarmathians, an extremist branch of the Ismaili sect, conquered much of the Tihāma and the plateau as far as San'a. The inhabitants of the plateau turned to the Zaidi Imam Yahya ibn Huseyn, called al Hadi ila al Haqq, for aid, but the Imam al Hadi's son, Mohammed was defeated and it was only few years later that his brother Naser Ahmed (died in 933) was able to prevail over the Qarmathians and drive them out of the country for good. During his reign, the Yemen was united from the Red Sea to Aden.
The Ismaili sect, to which the Qarmathians belonged, originated in the late 8th century and is one of the various manifestations of Shi'a. As we have already said, the Shiites recognised as their legitimate leader an Imam chosen from among the descendants of Ali. The sixth of these Imams had two sons, and the elder, Isma'il, was disinherited in favour of the younger. The Ismailis acknowledged Isma'il as the last legitimate Imam and evolved a doctrine based on an esoteric interpretation of the Koran. The Ismailis spread to various

countries in the Islamic world, including Egypt, where they appeared with temporal power in the second half of the 10th century, with the Fatimid dynasty.

Suleihids
The growth of Fatimid power in Egypt was reflected on the Yemen with the establishment of the Ismaili dynasty of the Banu Suleih.
Towards the middle of the 11th century the lord of Jabal Haraz (near Manākha), Ali bin Mohammed al Suleihi, succeeded in extending his power to include the whole of the Tihāma as far as Mecca and the plateau as far as San'a. The Zaidi Imam resisted in vain and was obliged to withdraw to the north of the country. The Suleihi sovereign acknowledged allegiance to the Fatimid caliph, sending him a rich display of gifts and offering to govern the country in his name. On the death of Ali al Suleihi, power passed to his son and a few years later to the latter's wife Sayyida Arwa bint Ahmed. Queen Arwa's reign marked a period of relative unity for the country and of constructive fervour in particular, the memory of which is still alive in popular tradition.

Hamdanids
When the Suleihi dynasty died out towards the end of the 11th century with the death of Arwa's son, the inhabitants of the plateau elected the sheikh of the Hamdan tribe as king, and he took the title of Sultan, choosing San'a as his capital. While San'a and the neighbouring territories were under the Hamdanid sultans, Sa'dah and Najrān continued to be ruled by the Zaidi Imam, while other small local

dynasties shared power in the rest of the country.

Ayyubids

In 1171 Salah ad Din Yusef bin Ayyub (Saladin the Great) deposed the last Fatimid sovereign whose vizier he was, and in the name of the caliph of Bagdad took it upon himself to reconvert Egypt from Ismaili heresy to Sunnite orthodoxy. In 1173, under the same religious pretext, he sent an expedition against the Yemen led by his brother Turan Shah, who conquered Zabīd, Aden, Ta'izz and finally San'a, putting an end to the Hamdanid dynasty.

Rasulids

For over half a century the Yemen was ruled by the Ayyubids. In 1229 the sixth of these, Nured Din Omar bin Ali Bin Rasul al Ghassani, declared himself independent and began the Rasulid (or Ghassanid) dynasty. For over two centuries, up to 1454, it dominated most of the country, reducing the territory subject to the Zaidi Imam to a tiny part in northern Yemen.

This dynasty marked the period of greatest splendour in Islamic Yemen: a large number of buildings still testify to the remarkable wealth and power of the Rasulid sovereigns, who embellished and fortified various cities. The capital Ta'izz became the centre of an intense artistic and cultural life. Many literary works and treatises on agriculture and medicine go back to this period, and many contemporary copper and silver objects witness a flourishing and refined craftmanship.

Tahirids

In 1454 a rebellion headed by Amer bin Taher overthrew the last Rasulid and gave rise to the Tahirid dynasty, whose main cities were Ta'izz, San'a and Rada'. The major mosques still in existence at Rada' date back to this period. In 1507 the Zaidi tribes elected Yahya Sharaf ed Din as Imam and he claimed religious sovereignty over the Tahirid king, Amer Abd al Wahhab.

Mamluks

When the latter refused to accept it, the Imam turned to the Mamluk Sultan of Egypt for aid and he, eager to conquer bases on the Arab coast of the Red Sea to offset the strong Portuguese commercial expansion, acknowledged the request and in 1516 sent an army into the Yemen. These troops, armed with guns which were at that time unknown to the people of the Arabian Peninsula, easily overcame Amer's army and soon conquered the whole Tihāma and the plateau as far as San'a. After defeating the Tahirids, the Mamluk troops turned against the Zaidis themselves. But with a successful campaign, Imam Sharaf ed Din managed to regain control first of San'a and then of the Tihāma. By forcing the Mamluks to leave the country he became the uncontested ruler of most of the Yemen.

First Turkish Conquest

In the meantime, important political changes which had taken place on the Mediterranean coast had strong repercussions on Yemeni history. By 1517 the Ottoman Sultan Selim I had conquered Egypt, carrying on the expansionist policy of the Mamluks in the Red Sea. A first military expedition, sent by Sultan Soliman the Magnificent in 1537, proved inadequate and was followed in 1559 by a second one supported by artillery. After various ups and downs, vainly contested by the Imam al Mutahhar, the Turks conquered almost all the country and placed it under the rule of a Turkish governor who took up residence in San'a. The Ottoman conquest, which lasted until 1636, was of great importance to the history of the Yemen. This, as a province of the Ottoman empire, emerges from its peripheral and isolated position to reflect the great splendour of the heyday of the Turkish civilization. The various governors nominated by the Sublime Porte stimulated cultural activity and promoted a great deal of public works: roads, canals and mosques were constructed. Thanks to this, Yemeni architecture was injected with new ideas and building techniques, and far from being spoilt, was enriched and developed.

The Turkish conquest did not mark the end of Zaidi resistence, and relations between the Turks and the Imam were punctuated with clashes and acts of friendship until, under the Imam Mu'ayyad Mohammed, the Turks left San'a and withdrew into the Tihāma. The position of the Turkish garrisons gradually became untenable. In 1636, the Sultan, instead of sending in more reinforcements as required, judged the occupation of the Yemen to be excessively expensive and ordered withdrawal from the country, so leaving it in the hands of the Imam Mu'ayyad Mohammed bin Qasim.

Imams of San'a

The Turkish withdrawal from the Yemen gave rise to a period of independence under the government of the Zaidi Imams, from now on also called "the Imams of San'a," as they had almost always kept this city as their capital. The long reigns of most of these Imams helped to ensure peace and prosperity in the country. The city of San'a owes much of its development to the Imam al Mutawakkil al Qasim, who ordered the building of the fortifications and palaces called the Mutawakkil, and to his grand-son al Mahdi Abbas who was responsible for a large number of public works and the building of the mosque named after him. It is worth recalling that it was during the reign of the Imam al Mahdi Abbas that the Danish explorer Carsten Niebuhr visited San'a and left a vivid description of the luxurious court of the Imam.

In the early part of the 19th century the country fell into anarchy, and various Imams were elected, all of whom were unable to exert any effective authority.

Second Turkish Conquest

In the 1840's the Yemen again attracted the Turkish government. It was thought necessary in Istanbul to occupy it, not only to gain tighter control of the Hijaz (the possession of Medina and Mecca being so important for religious prestige), but also to offset the policy of the English, who had been present in Aden since 1838. It should also be borne in mind that the interest of the Ottoman government in controlling the Yemen grew with the commercial importance the Red Sea acquired after the opening of the Suez Canal in 1869. The Turks had made their reappearance on the coast of the Yemen in 1849, when they tried to reassert their authority over the Zaidi Imam, demanding among other things that a detachment of 1500 soldiers be stationed at San'a. Following the extermination of this garrison, they temporarily gave up the idea of penetrating inland, and limited themselves to keeping the Tihāma, where a large number of garrisons were established. These garrisons provided

effective support when, in 1871, a new expedition, organised on a vaster scale and with the aim of subjecting the entire country, disembarked north of Hodeydah. These troops soon succeeded in conquering the hinterland as far as Manākha, where a delegation of officials from San'a surrendered the city and the entire plateau to the Turkish commander.

With the annexation of the Ta'izz and Asir regions, the Yemen was absorbed into the Ottoman empire, and after a long period of disorder acquired at least administrative unity. Its boundaries included almost the whole of modern Yemen with the exception of the northern mountainous region, still subject to the Imam, and the regions of Jawf, Ma'rib and Khawlān, whose tribes refused to accept Turkish domination. During their occupation the Turks had to tackle a series of violent revolts led by various Imams elected by the Zaidi populations, with neither of the sides managing to obtain a definite victory. The election of Imam Yahya ibn Mohammed in 1904 coincided with the conclusion of the lengthy and arduous negotiations by the Anglo-Turkish commission to establish the frontiers between the Yemen and the Aden protectorates. The struggle took on the character of a wholescale war of liberation. The first act of foreign policy by the new Imam was to denounce the Anglo-Turkish convention as an act without any legal value, since it had been ratified by two foreign powers during the temporary military occupation of Yemeni territory. The Imam then took it upon himself to establish the political and territorial unity of the country, and consequently to lead all the Yemeni people against the invaders, irrespective of any religious differences. The conflict

saw several reversals until the Imam won important political success with the treaty of Da'an in 1911, which acknowledged him spiritual and temporal leader over all the Zaidi, and established a ten-year truce. This state of affairs was to continue right up to the end of the First World War in 1918, when the collapse of the Ottoman empire caused the Turkish troops to leave the country for good.

Independence

In November 1918 Imam Yahya made his entry into San'a as independent sovereign.

The long reign of Imam Yahya ended in 1948 with his assassination by conspirators who occupied San'a and elected as Imam the leader of the plot, Sayyid Abdallah al Wazir. The crown-prince Ahmed, supported by northern tribes, succeeded in regaining power and after re-occupying San'a, he avenged his father's death with the massacre of over 3000 people. Once elected Imam, Ahmed transferred his capital to Ta'izz, where there was a sudden burst of building in the Aden style. After Ahmed's death in 1962, his son Mohammed al Badr was elected Imam, but was dethroned a few days later by a revolution against the Imamate led by some young officers. The Imam's flight from San'a, and his resistence with the support of the northern tribes, led to a civil war fanned by foreign governments and with the direct intervention of Egyptian troops. The war between Royalists and Republicans dragged on until 1969, when the two sides signed a lasting peace treaty and agreed to collaborate for the reconstruction of the country, which took the name of Yemen Arab Republic with its capital at San'a.

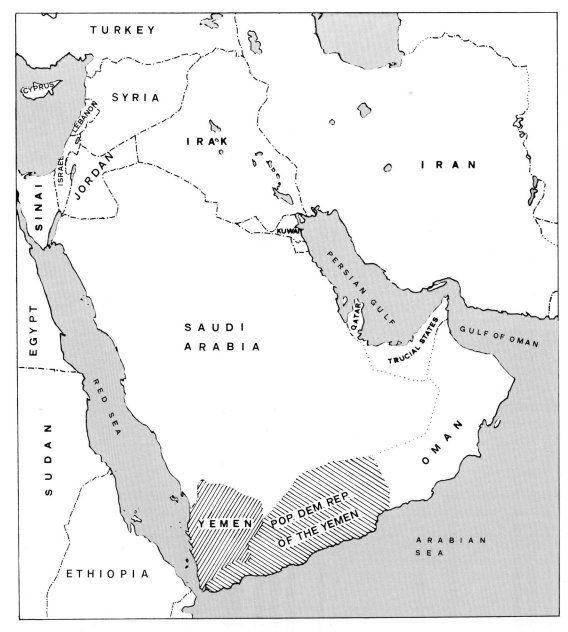

158. *Geographical position of Yemen in the Arabian Peninsula.*

159. *Map showing places of archaeological and artistic interest.*

TURKEY

CYPRUS

SYRIA

LEBANON

ISRAEL

JORDAN

IRAK

IRAN

SINAI

KUWAIT

PERSIAN GULF

QATAR

TRUCIAL STATES

GULF OF OMAN

EGYPT

SUDAN

RED SEA

SAUDI ARABIA

OMAN

YEMEN

POP DEM REP. OF THE YEMEN

ARABIAN SEA

ETHIOPIA

BIBLIOGRAPHY

Only works containing useful information for the study of architecture and town-planning in the Yemen during the Islamic period are mentioned here.

C. Niebuhr, *Voyage en Arabie*, Paris, 1776.

C. Niebuhr, *Description de l'Arabie*, Paris, 1779.

R. Manzoni, *El Yemen, tre anni nell'Arabia Felice*, Rome, 1884.

C. Rathjens, H. von Wissmann, Sanaa, *Zeitschrift der Gesellschaft für Erdkunde zu Berlin*, 1929, pp. 329-353.

C. Ansaldi, *Il Yemen nella storia e nella leggenda*, Rome, 1933.

S. Aponte, *La vita segreta nell'Arabia Felice*, Milan, 1936.

E. Rossi, *L'arabo parlato a San'a*, Rome, 1939.

E. Rossi, *Terminologia delle costruzioni nel Yemen*, A Francesco Gabrieli, Rome, 1964, pp. 351-357.

H. Scott, *In the High Yemen*, London, 1942.

C. Rathjens, *Jewish Domestic Architecture in Sana*, Jerusalem, 1957.

R. Lewcock, G.R. Smith, Two Early Mosques in the Yemen, *Art and Archaeology Research Papers* 1973, pp. 117-130.

R. Lewcock, G.R. Smith, "Three Medieval Mosques in the Yemen," pt. I & pt. II, *Oriental Art* 1974, I pp. 1-12, II pp. 1-12.

P. Costa, "La Moschea Grande di San'a," *Annali Istituto Orientale di Napoli*, 1974, pp. 487-506; plates I-XXX.

For a general bibliography on the Yemen see:
E. Macro, *Bibliography on Yemen and notes on Mocha*, Miami, 1960.

M. Wenner, *Modern Yemen, 1918-1966*, Baltimore, 1967.

CONTENTS